# How to Survive Life
# (and Death)

# How to SURVIVE LIFE (and Death)

## A Guide for Happiness in This World and Beyond

By Someone Who Died Three Times

### Robert Kopecky

Conari Press

First published in 2014 by Conari Press, an imprint of
Red Wheel/Weiser, LLC
With offices at:
665 Third Street, Suite 400
San Francisco, CA 94107
*www.redwheelweiser.com*

ISBN: 978-1-57324-636-1

Library of Congress Cataloging-in-Publication Data available upon
request.

Cover design by Robert Kopecky
Cover art © Robert Kopecky
Interior by Jane Hagaman
Typeset in Sabon

Printed on acid free paper in the United States of America.
EBM.
10 9 8 7 6 5 4 3 2 1
The paper used in this publication meets the minimum requirements
of the American National Standard for Information Sciences—Perma-
nence of Paper for Printed Library Materials Z39.48-1992 (R1997).

# Contents

*Dedicated to Dorothy, Ruth, Anne, Margaret, Sybil, Doris, and Susan . . . the feminine divine.*

*. . . and to Max, for his love and wisdom, who graciously consented to spend his life, and his last moments on this earth with us, showing us how to do it . . . and who remains a part of everything, and of us, forever.*

*"I'm not afraid to die, I just don't want to be there when it happens."*

Woody Allen

# Preface

Have you ever looked around one day to find that you were doing something you never imagined you'd be doing? Something you could never have foreseen in your wildest imagination? That's how I feel writing this book about things that no one wants to talk about, inspired by experiences I never dreamt of having. Experiences that no one in their right mind would ever want to have.

Then what could possibly compel me try to write a positive book about the one ultimate, undeniably negative experience in life—that is, the apparent end of it? How could a person ever become so easy, and even downright encouraging, about such an ominous and always-to-be-avoided subject as *dying*—much less speak with any authority about the one experience for which there's obviously so little first-hand expertise available? The answers to these questions might come more easily if I happened to be someone who'd had one of those remarkable Near Death (after-life) Experiences—and, not coincidentally, I am. In fact, as crazy as it sounds, I've had *three* of them.

Like a lot of people, I had my difficulties accepting all those Near Death Experience stories, until it happened to me—and then, oddly enough, even after it happened to me. For some deep-seated reason, I apparently couldn't face the powerful significance of my experiences; so, for years afterward, I kept pretending I was an agnostic concerning the critical questions of life and death, even though, in a very real way, I knew better. Even though my life had plainly and very painfully demonstrated a deeper truth to me over and over . . . and *over*.

I'm still not sure why it took such a long time to open up my mind to the truth imprisoned inside of me, to let it out and allow the fullness of it to start shaping my life. I guess it took whatever it took for me finally to become willing to look back at those experiences, accept them, *own* them, realize the truths that came out of each, and then try to live within the lessons they'd taught me about Life—based on what they'd taught me about death.

If you are a doubter, as I was, consider this: Of the now millions of people who, down through the ages, have claimed to have had an experience of *life after life,* thousands of the more recent cases have been very well documented. There are lots of very credible academic collections of case studies by extraordinarily well-qualified and dedicated experts like Elisabeth Kübler-Ross, Kenneth Ring, or Raymond Moody—and a host of others, if you're curious. Most of these cases have had so much in common with one another that they're clearly not just describing coincidental unconscious states a few survivors have reported, but what seem to be profound non-physical universal experiences that have been shared by so many people that they can be grouped into different distinct categories, levels, and types. So this isn't just some kind of urban legend we're exploring here. It's a bona fide human phenomenon—a real aspect of Life that's very possibly the opening experience of what happens when we make the transition we call dying.

As survivors of these experiences, are we all just a bunch of crackpots? Well, that would make for an awful lot of crackpots (always a distinct possibility). Are we all describing an actual passage into an extra-dimensional world that follows right on the heels of this one, or, as some would suggest, merely a complex set of vivid biochemical responses that everyone experiences as our common human form shuts itself down?

I don't think it matters much really, in cases like these. I know those suggestions don't bother me. I'm comfortably assured about the authenticity of my own vivid biochemical experiences and, in keeping with the testimony of all those other survivors, I know that something *more* definitely happens beyond this life, in a conscious world that's very different from, but just as real as, this one. Something that amounts to a continuation, a progression that we flow into seamlessly, immediately after we pass on from this world we think we know so well.

In light of all those people who've claimed to have had dramatic experiences beyond this life—who've supposedly died and then miraculously come back—my experiences didn't seem to me all that dramatic or miraculous. But that's kind of silly, isn't it? After all, they had to have been a little bit miraculous. So I do consider myself a member of that unusual club—perhaps even kind of a special member because, as I mentioned, I've actually had three such experiences in my life, of differing types. One of them was a momentary set of moving, dreamlike images; one was more grave—a struggle of sorts that took place over a number of hours; and one, my first and most profound of all, lasted a full day and apparently sent me off into an altogether different dimension of being.

I hope that I don't have any more such traumatic experiences for a good, long while—at least not until I'm really ready. Those three will do just fine for me, for the time being. I don't say that because the results of those transitions were all that terrible; in fact, they were mostly the opposite—after all, I'm still here to talk about them. It's just that the circumstances leading up to these experiences weren't what you'd consider a walk in the park—but then, I wouldn't expect that the circumstances leading up to Near Death Experiences ever are. Besides, it really isn't the sensations of nearly dying that I want to focus on at all; it's the way I think about life with a more complete understanding, from a perspective that came about as the result of those three extreme experiences. Perceptions change profoundly for anyone who has experienced the death of any loved one first hand—especially when it's his or her *own death*.

At different points in this book, I'll describe each of the incidents in my life as clearly as I can actually remember, without allowing my imagination to fill in what may be invented details. If you're looking for wondrous and fantastic descriptions of the afterlife, you won't really find them here. Because, while I respect and honor the more elaborate memories to which other survivors may bear witness, what I have held on to in the wake of death is the sense of a simpler wholeness and the belief that attempts to describe what the "afterlife" really is (including the little bit of it that I experienced) may be just the wishful machinations of our minds. Some reports may be more ecstatic, some more punitive; but how greatly they differ from one another suggests to me that they are creations of an individual nature. Despite how compelling many of them are, they may also simply be projections of our personal mentalities, imaginative obstacles of our strictly human nature that come between us and a greater reality.

My intention here is to try to share with you the benefits of what I've learned in a fairly direct and simple way—to avoid any effort to describe an indescribably different reality using the language and myth of our shared human reality. Believe me, there's already more than enough magic to go around.

Before and between these three experiences, I lived what might be called an interesting life. A rough childhood, punctuated by the deaths of all my grandparents by age twelve, and all of my aunts and uncles by my twenties. Most of them (my favorite aunt, Ruth, in particular) were lively, very funny people—mentors and protectors who showed me how a little well-placed humor could help to ease me through the difficult circumstances I'd been handed as a kid. Then it seemed they were suddenly all gone. I felt the foundations had slipped from under me.

In high school, I had wanted to be a doctor, but my first day of volunteering in a hospital gave me such a harsh introduction to the realities of mortality that I had to reconsider. On top of that, two young women with whom I was in relationships died early, tragic deaths. As a young person, deeply shaken by all that finality, I was at best full of questions about life and death and, at worst, full of cynical answers.

So I was always a roamer. I moved around a lot, restless and discontent, looking for something. Then, in an effort to "fix it," to find some meaning to my life, I got married at a very young age to another troubled young soul like myself. Naturally it didn't work. After seven years of marriage, my wife and I detached ourselves from our typical lives and started roaming together, traveling around the world for a year. Upon our return to America to resume our *normal* lives, I was suddenly and unexpectedly called to the bedside of my beloved Aunt Ruth, in time to witness the actual moment of her incomprehensibly unnecessary death, caused by malpractice.

Something happened to me then. From that point on, I just couldn't seem to gain a healthy purchase on life, despite outside appearances to the contrary. I became a bit unhinged in a way. My marriage ended, and I was cast off into an increasingly dangerous and destructive life that didn't lack for accomplishment or "success," but that wasn't satisfying or fulfilling in any real way—just achingly driven by skewed instincts. It took me many years of confusion— years of often unintentional survival (or of compassionate Providence)—to at last reach a moment of personal rebirth and transformation when I finally realized the much more comfortable way that Life had been showing me all along— the way to truly *live*.

I'd had to make a lot of hard choices, many of which I'd gladly take back if I could, in the course of searching without knowing what for. I'm sad to say that it was not a particularly conscious life I led, but rather one that repeatedly forced me to confront a succession of "unfair" consequences and injuries, including these experiences of a not-so-final end that I'd now like to share with you.

Since my two later Near Death Experiences weren't as lucid or transformative as the very first one, let me tell you about that one to start with. After all, it's the story that has profoundly, if sometimes unconsciously, underscored a good deal of the rest of my life, and it is what ultimately compelled me to set down all the ideas in this book. The understanding I have to offer you comes from these three stories, and this is the first of them.

I was in my mid-twenties, many years ago now. As I was prone to do as a young man, I was working way too much— maybe a hundred hours a week at two jobs. I always needed to keep my mind occupied back then, or I'd start feeling overwhelmed by worries and expectations. I always needed to feel as if I were going somewhere, getting somewhere; being where I was never felt like enough. My world seemed so intensely important to me at the time that I just plain overdid it and was badly "burned out"—a common enough malady at any time in our crazy culture.

My wife was taking a flight to visit her aunt, so I drove her to the airport late one afternoon. On the way home, at the end of another very long day, I passed an exotic-looking cocktail lounge that I'd passed before. It was one of those elaborate tiki-themed holdovers from the Sixties, with a lacquered bamboo façade and flickering torches that apparently proved irresistible. I've always loved that stuff. I stopped in for a cocktail, thinking: What could it hurt? I guess I didn't think it would hurt one bit, and so I unconsciously rewarded myself for all of my recent work and worry. But, as wrung-out as I was, I'm sure the two tall, exotic drinks I had contributed in no small measure to the tragedy, or near-tragedy, that followed.

Driving home as it approached darkness, I turned down an unfamiliar street that I imagined to be a straight and easy shortcut home. I was going about thirty-five or forty miles an hour when something happened that you don't see all too often anymore. My car stereo *ate* the cassette tape that I was playing, making that bloopy, robotic sound that we used to dread in those days. I'm sure those kinds of small equipment issues are common causes of single-car accidents, and so it definitely was in my case. The very last "real" thing I remember was pulling the cassette out—a long, fettucine-like strand of tape snagged in the tape player's mechanism—and then suddenly *the lights went out.*

The next thing I knew, the very next instant, I was near the top of a telephone pole, looking down over the street below. Right next to me was a bright white streetlight illuminating the scene, a couple of moths circling frantically around it. There beneath me was the car I had been driving, seriously smashed into that same telephone pole, front end caved in, hood crumpled and popped open, and steam roiling up into the light. There was hissing and pinging, and I heard voices and saw lights snap on in the neighborhood houses. People began running out to see what had happened. I heard them crying out with alarm, calling back to their houses to get help. "Get an ambulance; this looks bad!" someone yelled out.

I tried to get their attention, to tell them I was fine and that they didn't need to worry, but from where I stood (or sort of floated), they were all busily behaving as if there were a real emergency going on. And besides, it seemed as if no one down there could see me or hear me anyway.

The windshield was smashed outward in one of those big tempered-glass spider-web shapes, and there was someone's arm hanging out of the open window, with the other arm looped through the mangled steering wheel. I couldn't quite see the victim's face from where I was, but I knew who it was down there below, motionless. Hot water poured out of the fractured radiator and ran into the dark fluid on the ground that I suspected was blood—that I realized, in fact, was *my* blood.

But the whole time, I was actually just fine—in fact, *better* than fine, up there floating just above all the activity. There was absolutely no pain, just a profound sensation of comfort and ease—and no sense of time at all, or of gravity.

Then the ambulance arrived. People described to the police what they'd heard and seen. I eavesdropped up above them a little bit, but had a little trouble focusing on what they were saying. And then it was time for me to go.

*I was not alone.* I knew that I had been joined by a benevolent presence, positioned just out of view, a little above and to the left behind me. The presence began prompting me to move along, and gently shepherded me out over the scene, away into what I can only describe as a bank of soft, gray cotton-wool fog of sorts. The action beneath me diminished, like a film fading out. I was light—weightless, warm, and very comfortable—and I felt completely free and at peace, a feeling I'd never experienced before then, and only in little bits since.

Then I remember being in a place that seemed lovely—perhaps a bit pastoral and indistinct, but altogether very agreeable. I was engaged in a pleasant but quite serious conversation of sorts. Though I don't really remember the content of it, or even actually speaking out loud, I have always felt it was a long, intense session that I wasn't supposed to remember in its entirety—a conversation in which lots of very important things got hashed out. It carried on pleasantly, in an easy, slightly business-like manner for an indefinable time, like a familiar kind of interview. Then it ended.

That was all I remember of that period, which, as it happened, turned out to be about eighteen hours in actual physical time. I regained consciousness briefly once, as I was being moved from one hospital to another to take advantage of the University plastic surgeon's residency there, but I soon slipped back into unconsciousness for what turned out to be a much longer time than I'd thought.

Sadly, that nice little car was a total loss. I'd caved the steering wheel into a whacky loop with my face and smashed the windshield with my head, despite having had my shoulder harness on . . . so naturally I was not in such good shape either. Finally, late the next day, I returned to consciousness, alone in a quiet hospital room. I had quite a severe concussion, but otherwise the prognosis was good, all things considered. I knew there was some other way I'd been changed, however, although I couldn't really see how yet. I just wished it had never happened. I did know that I had a slightly different face and a serious, heartfelt apology to make to my wife. It was actually her car that I'd wrecked.

A couple of days later, I returned to the accident scene, my head still all bandaged up, and examined what I thought I had seen—what I could only have seen from my vantage point up by the streetlight. I surveyed the areas behind hedges and around the sides of the houses, and checked the angles up and down to the crash site. Everything I couldn't see from the ground *was just as I had seen it* from my place up near the top of the telephone pole—the shape of the street light, side doors and trash cans, back fences, and the like. It all checked out.

Of course the obvious lesson I learned right away was: Don't drink and drive at all, ever. And always drive as if your life depended on it, because it does. Even if you think you're plenty sober, you may not be quite sober enough. It's not all up to your best judgment. There are a lot of converging dynamic forces we are constantly subject to when we drive, just as when we live.

As I mentioned before, for some reason it actually took many more years for me to open up to the deeper meaning that this experience eventually brought to life inside of me. I apparently suppressed the incident—part of some kind of psychic self-defense, I suppose—until a number of years later, after my two other brushes with death had occurred.

Eventually, the meaning and power of these experiences began to percolate—to rise up and spread through me—and then began slowly, undeniably to inform (and re-form) my life from the inside out. It seems I had to be broken open over and over again by Life, physically and psychically, until the meaning of those memories crystallized within me and a conversion of sorts could take place. And then I came to know with absolute certainty the lesson of that first experience with mortality: that *I am a spiritual being having a physical life experience,* and that our actual transition from this life to the next (and possibly from the former) is seamless, relatively painless, and full of warmth, assurance, and ease . . . as I now believe most of Life is actually meant to be.

Unfortunately though, I did have to be there when it happened.

So, that's my opening story. I hope it tells you a little something about what's motivating me, and how I came to my cautiously positive view of what's generally considered to be the ultimate not-so-positive experience of our lives. It didn't come easily, and I most certainly don't recommend such violent and dramatic means as what occurred to me in this and my other two stories.

I suppose one of my goals is to spare you the extremes I went through to gain the simple understandings that I've acquired about life and change and pain and loss—and particularly about death, which, as I found out for myself, is most definitely *not* an ending, but instead a compelling and miraculous passage. On the other side of the same coin, I've gained a rather unique perspective on the nature of Life that I think may have helped me discover some very practical sources of wholeness and happiness with a clarity that I would never have considered possible before. A really good, hard kick in the pants can do that for you.

What slim authority I may have to tackle some of the bigger-than-life themes I hope to address in this book comes only from having been there myself. All the observations and advice I'll give you are based on the particularly hard-to-come-by information my life has given me—advice which, while sincerely offered, doesn't necessarily mean I'm right about everything. I learned some hard lessons by definitely having wandered down *the road best not taken* a few too many times. I only hope the recognition of these imperfections will help to validate the practicality and sincerity of my suggestions. You can learn a lot by getting it wrong.

There may also be a number of moments when you'll find yourself thinking: "That's easy for him to say." Most likely, however, they'll be the moments when it's not.

While this may not be a book for the already-convinced, as it were—that is, for avid followers of established religious or other spiritual conclusions—I do believe there's something important here for everyone. If you already have your beliefs well in place, and are comfortable with them where they are, my hat is off to you. I only ask that you keep an open mind. Though I won't be dealing with questions of religion, inevitably a good deal of my life-and-death experiences will cross over into that territory—territory that, from my perspective, is shared by everyone, no matter where they come from or what they believe. What I've drawn from Life and death doesn't discriminate; everyone is welcome.

I apologize ahead of time that this book is not at all about the legalities of anything. There's no discussion of wills or estates or taxes or insurance policies—nothing like that here. When it comes to your dying, I do recommend that you keep honest and current with the serious legal affairs that affect your partners in life; take care of all the arrangements that are important to everyone surviving you. You wouldn't want to drop the complications of an entire life into the lap of an unsuspecting loved one, or to have your intentions completely misunderstood after you're gone (or especially while you're still here). I'm not at all qualified to give you advice about your legal affairs—not in the same way that I'm qualified to talk about finding happiness, or how to make things a bit more right, or how to get beaten up and still bounce back. This is a little different kind of *how-to* book.

You may find my inadvertently earned resilience sometimes comes off as a bit too direct. Getting past the rough stuff has simplified my life that way. This is simply meant to be a book about what you can do in this life to help you along the way with some grace, some ease, and maybe some fun—and to help you look forward to and prepare for what may very well be coming next. One of the central beliefs that I'll return to over and over comes from the old adage: Life doesn't happen to you; it happens *for you*. To take that a bit further, as I hope to do, I believe the same most certainly holds true for death.

Since it was the quality with which I lived my life that definitively influenced not just the ways in which I left it, but also what I carried along with me into "that undiscover'd country," you'll find that a lot of what's here isn't so much about dying as it is about living *well*—that is, the approaches and preparations that will make for an easier today and tomorrow, and so ever after too. Since I believe that dying really *is living as well,* this is actually a single-purpose primer of sorts, informed by the experiences of someone who has (unintentionally) done a little bit of each.

So please bear with me if I ever seem flippant. I'm not really. I take my dying (and anyone else's) deadly seriously. It's just that, in order to negotiate this mortal roller coaster, I believe that you need to have a sense of humor about *everything*—including death, taxes, and, in my own case, "skinheads" and crocodiles.

Especially crocodiles.

All of us have stood on the edge of a vast starry sky, gazed at the moon, and wondered: Just what in the heck is really going on here? I can tell you from my experiences that what we normally consider to be "the end" is more than likely the passageway into a world where all the answers to those previously unanswerable questions can be found. A world that's formed, in part anyway, by the experiences, the understanding, and the life that we carry along into it.

You see, it really isn't about dying; it's about living *more* Life, where Life is a long trip that doesn't quite stop at death.

So then, if I may, I'd like to take you on a little adventure into it, around it, and *through* it—if you can spare me just a bit of your precious time and give me the benefit of whatever doubts you may still have.

And away we go . . .

# An Introduction to Aloha— Saying Hello and Goodbye

The opening quote from Woody Allen pretty much sums up what many of us really think about dying—when we actually get around to thinking about it, that is. It is, after all, inevitable, and actually happening all around us all the time, but who in their right mind wants to dwell on it? It's the one thing that everybody does, and that everybody wants to do as easily, as painlessly, and as well as possible. But since we seldom discuss just how it is that you go about doing that, it seems as if dying may be a good place to start for a change.

Chances are that as you get older—or if you're just a soul with a questioning nature—you may find yourself coming to a point where avoiding the subject of death seems a little immature, or even superstitious. This is the point at which you may want to forget whatever taboos there are, and just talk about it for a change. Maybe even to do a little investigation of the personal and cultural attitudes that make us feel so much fear about what's really such a commonplace and unavoidable occurrence, without all the mandatory doom and gloom.

Could it be that we avoid it because we feel as if it's always too soon to consider what we still may have to make up for? All that rich potential lost, or repentance yet to seek? Or maybe we fear we'll never be able to produce enough character—that we won't be able to summon up what it takes to help a loved one when the time comes, or to meet that daunting challenge ourselves. Is it mostly just the *pain* that we're afraid of? That seems like a reasonable enough concern to me, all right. Like most folks, I am only in favor of pain philosophically—as an unavoidable, strictly temporary learning device, that is.

Believe me, I had never planned on personally investigating the nature of death. Like most of us, however, I didn't have much choice in the matter, or I would have chosen "Not now, thanks" of course. Then, when I discovered for myself that it all appears to be part of the same big process—that dying *is living* and living *is dying*—I began to develop a perspective of continuity and a kind of strategy that could help me in living *this* life. Suddenly, I began to see how that perspective can give us an entirely different, easier, and more relaxed attitude toward the whole subject.

What I'm getting at is that this conversation doesn't need to be nearly as bad as it sounds—although it does sound pretty bad, I'll grant you that. The fact is that I'm (obviously) always quite happy to talk about death nowadays, although I've found I do need to be a little bit careful about when and where I do that. For example, a birthday dinner for an in-law is usually not the right time; likewise, it can be a pretty tough sell around people who are particularly sensitive, dramatic, or terribly fearful about death. Most folks need to be sensibly pragmatic and open or spiritually fit and ready—or *both*—to be willing to enter into any kind of self-examination, particularly when it is of such a traditionally delicate nature.

With those people for whom a death is a recent or more imminently approaching fact, please join the conversation only if you're comfortable with it. And even if you're not entirely comfortable, keep in mind that this is intended to be a much more positive, much less morbid, and (since the two are not exclusive) more realistic and even *magical* conversation than any other you'll ever hear on the subject. Along with the unavoidable hard parts, I'll be trying to address death as an enlivening, extra-dimensional right of passage from a point of view that admittedly may seem a little loosely wound to you at first.

So let me try to ground the discussion in the obvious from the get-go.

Obviously, dying is happening to everybody you've ever heard of, and everybody you've never heard of. You, me, everyone you've ever known or will ever know. It's a process that's happening on slightly different schedules to everyone living, all the time. In fact, there are about a zillion people, from the most famous to the not-at-all-famous, who have made this simple transition during our lifetimes, or are making it *right at this very moment*. It is a constant, regular, ongoing fact of life we will all get to know. On that grander scale, it's really not such a big deal. On the scale of you and me, it really is a pretty big deal.

Of course, just living itself brings up plenty of those less-than-entirely comfortable questions, doesn't it? Some we eventually get good answers to, some we don't. Questions like: Why am I here? Why are we here? What is this really all about? Or: What happens to us when we die? Where do we go? And most important for the purposes of this book: Is there a really good way to go about living to prepare for our "end" and what comes next? Could there possibly be any *good* way to die? It seems clear that some people definitely do have "better," more satisfactory deaths than others. So, how can we make the whole process easier, in a way that will hopefully provide us with the best, well . . . results?

These are serious questions you may ask that deserve to be asked, and discussed, and even answered—if at all humanly possible.

We'll have to start somewhere if we want to make sense of all these elusive mysteries, struggles, and strategies of (living and) dying. The goal is to deflate our unavoidable fears vigorously and rationally, and to try to supply some good answers about just what is going on here and what it all entails—right up until we go—as well as how we may even want to go about it in the best fashion possible. How do we get ready for "the end," even if, God forbid, it happens to be tomorrow? And after all, who knows?

My own unexpected Near Death Experiences (NDEs for short) put everything in a new context for me, and made me replace a lot of our common assumptions about dying and about preparing for death—all those typically solemn considerations, attitudes, and arrangements that supposedly must be observed, but that don't really have all that much to do with what's happening here and now. As death is part of a continuing cycle of Life, our approach has to be more about where we are in this life in every moment, and so where we *will be*—especially if we find our time is suddenly a lot shorter than we had expected it to be. Or especially if it's not.

I realized it all required adopting a different perspective, one that included not only my brief views from the other side, but also a somewhat radically different approach to living life in general. I say somewhat because, for many people, nothing I suggest will seem like a stretch at all. For others, however, it may seem very radical indeed, and it will need to be to break open the old frozen status quo and force the creation of a more practical and effective way to live. For me, it meant embracing the new reality I'd been given by revising some basic fears and assumptions I'd had about death—and, less obviously, about life as well.

For example, consider this twist, if you will: As scary as dying may seem to us, it really isn't as scary as being born. It just doesn't feel that way because we have so much time to think about dying. But consider, if you will, all the momentous determinations that are happening to us when we're being born. Didn't you ever wonder why most babies come into this world screaming and crying with such heart-felt conviction? What do they know that we seem to have forgotten? A doctor may suggest that it's just because they need to start their lungs functioning, but couldn't that be done just as well by laughing hilariously? You don't see that very often, do you? Babies laughing out loud when they're born? Not nearly as often as you see a seasoned old soul calmly and blissfully "passing away."

Or just imagine being a teenager; return to the mental state you were in then. I dare you. Some folks may relish the opportunity. I would personally find it absolutely ter-rifying—like driving a race car with no steering. That's one thing I feel Life got totally backward. It would be fine if old age and death came along before you'd learned all that much about Life, but wouldn't it have been nice to have had a little more preparation for being a teenager? To have known a good deal more about Life and all its romantic ramifications *prior* to the onset of so momentous a chal-lenge as *puberty*? After all, it is an awful lot for a relative newcomer to have to deal with.

Since it's likely that nothing ahead can be all that much worse than the scariest parts of life that you've gotten through already, and since most of us have suffered plenty of serious slings and arrows and experienced our fair share of *fear* by now, you needn't be afraid of how to handle an uncertain future, or of leaving unfinished business behind. Those are issues that can be addressed fairly easily in a few simple steps. So, since it is probably always "downhill from here" in any number of ways, you can know with assurance in your heart that many of the hardest parts of your life are already behind you. There's always going to be a couple of somewhat difficult bumps in the road ahead, but not like anything you haven't seen before in one form or another. The same themes simply recur in a slightly different arrangement. It may look like new territory because you haven't been through that specific experience yet. But still, it's all in the course of *Life* with all its very familiar complications.

Dealing with the death that's in all of our futures appears to be the one really difficult commitment we all share, because it seems so frighteningly different from anything else in our lives. But what I'm saying is that *it isn't*. When it happened to me, it actually felt very familiar. And unlike many of the difficult situations I've had to meet in my life, once I was into it, it was not hard at all. It was very easy and surprisingly comfortable. Mind you, it was still an unexpected challenge, but not at all as bad as many of life's continuing difficulties can be—like going to court or having oral surgery, for example. In fact, dying felt like a substantial relief, and I didn't really even have much of anything wrong with me. Two out of the three times, I was perfectly healthy. In fact, my life was not-so-bad to quite good. But even at that, "dying" felt like having a big weight removed from my shoulders.

So, while we all know theoretically that dying is a relief—even "liberating," so to speak (especially if you're suffering)—it's still not something we want to do. Naturally, we all want to live. But one thing I do want to suggest strongly is this: Compared to some things, death is not nearly as bad as you may think it is.

It won't be easy, and it will be sad, and it will inspire painful feelings of powerlessness and loss. In short, it's certainly nobody's idea of a good time. But if we can just agree that much of Life definitely *is* a good time, and if dying is really just a particularly difficult part of living, then we can try considering all of the things that have made the difficult parts of life more bearable, even enriching. Many of the same realizations, approaches, and principles that have seen us through the hard times before and made life happier and more fulfilling will work the same way for us as we navigate through our most careful and mysterious challenges. Maybe there's a little of that *real* magic that can help us out too.

# Why Me—
# and Everybody Else?

It's hard not to take it personally. The "terminally unique" aspect of dying seems pretty well justified. It really doesn't matter how many people do it; it's still just happening to you, or to me, or to someone we care about. And there is an inevitable sense of unfairness to the ending of anything we cherish. Especially *life,* and especially if it seems to be ending before its time. Or not.

Since we're all part of this same mysterious system, there's a frequently asked question that could be posed by any of us at either end of life, in hopes that we'd get some kind of an answer: Why? *Why me*—here and now? Why is this whole crazy mechanism wound up the way it is, allowed to collect all that speed and momentum, and then left to fall apart slowly and shut down? Or to end with some totally inappropriate unforeseeable abruptness? What is that all about?

Well, my NDEs all pointed me to three simple possibilities really: *expression, evolution,* and *Love.*

Not expression—as in having to do something brilliant or in some way to become hugely important—but *expression*—as in finding out who you really are and being *that*. Finding your true, authentic self, and what real meaning your life is meant to have—even if it's "only" to you, or "only" to be there for somebody else—and finding the positive nature of that self-expression, whatever it may be.

I don't mean evolution as in "the theory of," but instead *evolution* as in the process of evolving *spiritually*—that personal and collective motivation to keep growing and expanding above and beyond all the day-to-day stuff, right on through this life to whatever comes next. To rise above the human noise and find a path to our higher selves through a realization of the Eternal that is our real nature.

I don't mean love as simple sentimentality, but rather *Love* as the most powerful underlying energy and strategy for living, and for all Life—as the single most effective counteractive force to the subconscious self-sabotage that can be active in each of us, and in our society. Simply put, I mean Love as being the true medium of Life.

Absolutely everything, including ourselves and everything around us, is, in one way or another, an expression of the magical consciousness that energizes everything that exists. I'm sorry to get magical on you so soon, but I for one don't see how it can be avoided while we're all *sitting on a planet in outer space*. We've all seen the wonderful, mysterious, provocative, sometimes ghastly things that the world can be. We all know the delightfully indescribable beauty of nature or childhood, and the senseless horrors of inhumanity and environmental degradation. We've all been amazed by the remarkable ingenuity of our man-made wonders. For the most part, this does appear to be a world of reason, with reasonable explanations for everything. Or at least it's comfortable to think so.

But what about the way the moon just hangs in the sky like a shiny dime, when we all know that it's really a massive ball of cheese? Answer me that. Even "the empirical truth" of it all, even *science*, is nothing if not a magic act—first convincing us that we know exactly what the world is, and then suddenly changing what "exactly" is right in front of our eyes, over and over and over again. Our science has gotten very good at describing the vastness of time and space, and the incomprehensibly tiny world of molecules and sub-atomic particles and the like, but everything in between is made up from millions of years of shared, unfathomable consciousness, and can only really be described consistently by mystics, poets, artists, children, or others who are, on occasion, considered to be completely out of their minds.

We're swimming in this magic always, from our opening cry to our closing sigh. And here we all are, just this one little point, this smudge, this rocket burst that is *I Am*. The flower at the end of this particular stem. I'm just a dad or a sister or a friend. I'm this building, this concerto, this register ringing, this real estate deal, *this book*. That's what I am meant to express—this one little piece, or part, of Life. Seven billion little pieces of everything, and counting.

As for the reason . . . well, it's an *evolution* that we're taking part in. Personally and collectively. An evolution of the larger spiritual expression that all Creation seems to be—as much as we can know from the little bit of it we can perceive, which apparently isn't all that much. But even from that little bit, it appears that everything, including you and yours truly, is growing along its own line toward a kind of perfection, or apparent demise (or transformation)—which is a kind of perfection in itself, because it contributes perfectly to the continuity and expression of everything that came before, and everything that will follow.

Just as when you leave that house you lived in for so long and new people move in and fix it up, or nobody does and it gets knocked down and they put in a new office or a museum or a public garden. Then it becomes a new part of the world, just for now. Or you leave your business to your son, so that maybe he'll carry on and define his life with it in the same way that you did; but then he sells it and becomes a massage therapist or a cartoonist—as he always wanted to be. Then that little change becomes another new part of the world as well. The last leaf left from the autumn is pushed out by the new growth in spring, and new flowers blossom into being, and even the world is constantly blossoming into its new self.

So we're compelled to ask: Why? Well, it's pretty simple, as big explanations go—so you can blossom and become yourself. So you can learn to be your true, timeless (possibly even *interdimensional)* self—separate from cultural and material superficialities. So you can learn to contribute to life, to participate in the cycle of Love and creation and growth that reaches across life, across time. In short, so you can learn what you can contribute and how you can evolve personally and spiritually—and in those ways, to play your part in the evolution of everything. So death, too, is really one of your ultimate contributions—a transition into your next divine expression.

What if you're facing death—your own or that of someone you love—and it seems to have arrived much sooner than it should? Isn't there an irrefutable injustice in that? Yes, there may be; but Life's sense of justice has invisible roots. It may seem that there hasn't been a real chance yet for enough evolution and expression in a life that ends prematurely, but what do we really know? *This* is how long we live, after all; so *this* is how long we're supposed to live. It still may not feel fair, but it could be that the too-short life you're mourning has already contributed much more than you'll ever know just by having been lived. We are incapable of knowing how far our lives have reached, and are always reaching, out into the world. Really.

If you find yourself facing the unfairness of death, you have a choice. You can spend the remaining time believing that you're being cheated of something more that you deserve to get from life—that you're the victim of cruel fate. Or you can simply continue living through it as well and as meaningfully as you possibly can, deactivating your fears and regrets. Take a look at all the miracles that Life has already been, and always is. What if you knew it wasn't all over with *this*, after all?

When you take that approach, then nothing is ever over. You may very well discover that the thing you thought you were missing is really alive in any moment, and in every moment. Then you'll be given the clarity to recognize victimhood as a form of selfishness, and Life as the miraculous, never-ending magic that it is. A magic as "simple" as the sun rising and setting, and rising again. Don't worry that it may get very dark, because it always will; but then it really always is "the darkest just before the dawn." That's the moment when miracles usually happen, or we wouldn't call them miracles.

Does calling it selfish to feel like a victim seem unfairly critical and idealistic at a painful time? Well, maybe it is; but it's also the door to a very effective strategy for helping to remove a lot of the sadness and pain in any hurtful experience. Mostly the *psychological* pain, I mean. It goes something like this.

The times in life when we're the most selfish and self-centered are usually the most painful as well—particularly psychologically and spiritually painful, that is. The less self-centered we become, the less pain we experience—and the less we inflict.

Have you ever noticed how some people go through really terrible things without a lot of drama and still care enough to ask how *you're* doing, while the ones who complain and expect sympathy the most appear to care very little about anyone else and seem to revel in their pain and even to be intent upon generating more of it for others? When we complain, we become obstacles to the kind of positive human exchange that benefits everybody—especially ourselves.

If you do your best simply to be of positive use to others, to contribute with your attitudes and actions right now, whatever your situation is, it will literally help to no end. Being of service to others may not take all the hurt away, but it is an action, in fact *a strategy,* that helps more than anything else can in amazing ways.

Sometimes there just doesn't seem to be any reason why bad things have to happen to us; but it is inescapable, isn't it? Usually, it is for some good reason that's just hard for us to see at first, or maybe for some good reason we'll never be able to see. Then usually the bad stuff isn't nearly as bad as we expect it to be and, as clichéd as it may sound, most often ends up being something we learn from—if we're paying attention, that is. It becomes part of our invisible evolution. And, as an answer to that selfish sense of victimhood, it gives us the ability to turn the pain around and demonstrate to other people how well they may be able to get through the same mess simply by sharing our experience and advice with them.

Naturally, it's all in the way you energize a situation. If you want to make it bad, brother, you can make it bad. But if you just relax and pay attention while you're going through what seems to be a bad situation, you'll often discover that there's even something kind of fascinating about it. Something remarkable, maybe even beautiful, that you never noticed before because you always tried so hard to avoid it. Something transformative. Even if it is really, truly bad, having that flexible, open attitude will still make it easier to get through the discomfort and hard feelings to the other side, and then to go on more easily from there.

As simple as it sounds, being negative about any experience in life makes it more difficult; being as positive as possible makes it easier. But you knew that already. Positive people survive more, because they've *got more Life.* Positivity expands; negativity collapses. That's a basic lesson of Spiritual Fitness 101.

And take heart—because even in the worst of times, there's still that whole wonderful, mysterious dimension of "magic" going on behind the scenes that we simply can't know about, yet. Unimaginable, unseen, miraculous aspects of Life about which we haven't any clue. We've all experienced it—that magic—with a crazy, coincidental phone call out of nowhere, or an old friend appearing in an impossible place at an impossible moment. Or with that friend or relative whose diagnosis gives them six months to live, but then they experience an inexplicable reversal of the condition and live forty years longer than they're supposed to.

From just the little bit I've seen, coincidences and miracles like these are only the tip of that magical iceberg.

Even science has proven the existence of the paranormal so definitively that we absolutely know it exists—through study after endless study, many held to much higher standards than typical research demands due to the controversial nature of the subject. It just seems hard, in our mechanical role as human beings, to allow all that mystery—all that magic—into the "reality" of our lives.

Well, I feel as if I've gotten off to a pretty fast start, since I've got us asking *Why me?* already and delving into the paranormal. Before I get down to the nuts (and I do mean nuts) and bolts, maybe I should back up and get a little more of that magical Universe out of the way first. So let's go back to where I guess it all started—with a great big *bang.*

# So What's the Matter?

In this chapter, I'm going to get very deep, very profound. Philosophical, even. I'm going to put out as much "Big Picture" wisdom as I can muster. I'm going to try to tie cosmology, metaphysics, and quantum reality together with my spiritual experiences and my larger themes in a coherent and compelling way. It's going to be one of the shortest chapters in the book.

In order to get this deep, we have to start out in deep space, where the entire Milky Way galaxy looks like just another lustrous, twinkling pinwheel of stars and space dust. Somewhere out in the outer third of the spiral there's a little out-of-the-way solar system, the center of which is the smallish star we call our Sun. As we push closer in, past some swirly, gassy planets and past a couple of bald, rocky ones, we approach the little blue ball that is our Earth. We stop and take a look at it, at arm's length. Through the marbleized cloud cover, we see the continents with their greens and tans, the white polar ice caps, and, if we look very very closely, we may barely perceive a faint five-o'clock shadow of darkish fuzz concentrated in numerous tiny locations. That's *us*—that's humanity, looking a bit like traces of moss or mold on our little blue ball.

The whole of living consciousness, so far as we know, is concentrated in that tiny layer roughly between the top surface of the Earth's crust and the very bottom elevations of the atmosphere. This layer, in its totality, is comparatively thinner than the lacquer on a globe—on a sphere that's to scale, far smoother than a billiard ball—whose mountains would dwarf the Himalayas, relatively speaking. Within the scant limitations of this seemingly insignificant space in the Universe there exists, and has ever existed, everything significant that we know or have ever known of Life, aside from possible rudimentary fossil traces seen on a few Martian rocks.

Inside this tiny film of existence, waves and sub-atomic particles of matter coalesce into all the life and substance that we know. Constantly changing in a largely closed energetic system, matter forms and re-forms itself into you, me, everybody, all the animals and plants, the water and rocks and dirt, all the buildings and machinery and power—all the everything that will ever be evolving as an expression of collective and personal consciousness alive on our actively *living* planet. This perpetually evolving "reality" serves as the ever-shifting medium of all new manifestations of quantum consciousness that the Earth will ever bear witness to. Whew!

In view of this inescapable reality, it seems a bit self-centered to consider ourselves as anything too terribly separate or different from anything else around us, everything that shares our very same elemental composition. Does moss consider itself special and one of a kind, at an independent cellular level? Probably not nearly as much as we do. But if you look at moss very closely, every single cell appears to be from ordinarily to gorgeously to grotesquely unique—just like all of us "independent" human cells . . . with some even a little more unique than others.

From that all-encompassingly objective point of view, it's not so hard to imagine that there could be a single energizing and animating Source behind it all, giving life and form to everything in our sphere of existence and beyond. Something infinitely larger than all of us and everything put together, driving all that evolution and expression of matter and energy throughout the Universe, and precipitating all the creation and destruction on our little planet. If that infinite *source spirit* enlivens everything and everyone, then I am a small expression of it myself, and you are too—apart from our ever-changing material form (with my form ever changing mostly in all the wrong directions).

I believe it's just an inkling of this unfathomable experience of Life that my personal near-death episodes allowed me to glimpse. Having peeked around that corner a couple of times has given me the basis of my understanding that I am actually that weightless, activating spiritual component—separate from the body that I'm in—and that I will continue to be that after this body wears down and calls it quits. That's the understanding I'm trying to pass along—that dual context for our lives: the dense, physical, material part that happens here, full of the change and sensation and struggle that accompanies all this creation and destruction (in short, the part that pays rent); and the light-as-air part that continues on into a largely unknown, but apparently easy, state of grace and serenity—if we work through things well enough here, that is.

That's the idea underlying every insight I have in this book. So if you think that the premise is absurd or impossible, don't take this the wrong way, but I believe you have a critically informative experience to look forward to—and I'm sure you'd agree, if you'd been along with me to see those little pieces of it for yourself.

# Are We on a Honky-Tonk Merry-Go-Round?

There's a famous true story about a man named James Flowerdew (what a great name!) who was watching a BBC documentary about the ancient city of Petra in Jordan on his "telly" one day. Suddenly, he realized that he recognized the place the archeologists in the film were excavating. He knew right where they were, without ever having been there, from his chair in England. He contacted the BBC, who aired the program, and was put in touch with the archeological team from the documentary. What he told them about the ancient city seemed to be so accurate that they arranged for him to travel to the archeological site in Jordan. When he got there, he proceeded to direct their excavations with an amazing knowledge of the various specific locations, buried for nearly 2,500 years, complete with details like where he used to work and what all the different spaces and rooms had been used for. Everything he told them made perfect sense, and fit their subsequent discoveries with an accuracy that was impossible to explain—save for one explanation.

There are people who can describe villages a half a world away, exactly as they were hundreds of years ago. Children who, when they first begin to talk, spontaneously recall all the members of a family who lived in a faraway town years before they were born, the house they lived in, who their neighbors were, and even which member of the family they had been themselves. When the existing records are checked, it's all found to be completely accurate.

Thousands of such examples have been recorded. I don't know why they aren't better known or celebrated, as you would think they should be. I'm not sure why we don't seem to be able to acknowledge the profound implications of these kinds of cases. I suppose it's for the same reason that I was unable to recognize the significance of my Near Death Experiences for so long. Sometimes we just don't seem to be able to believe in any other reality than the one we're experiencing right now. But then, all these peoples' experiences were reality too—maybe even more so.

How to Survive Life (and Death)

Reincarnation is a given fact of Life in many systems of belief, but it's strangely resisted in modern Western culture. Perhaps that's because our Western egos have so much at stake in definitively attributing everything we are and can become to just this one little old life. Or maybe it's because our religious leaders are satisfied with the order of things they provide us with. I don't know for sure. What I *do* know for sure is that reincarnation, or the concept that our lives continue before and after this one, is believed in and prepared for in Buddhism, Hinduism, Islam, Jainism, and other ancient and modern religious traditions. Though it played a part in Christianity's early formation, it was "officially" rejected, in spite of it being the apparent point of it all, it would seem—that is, *resurrection,* and an expansive life in the great hereafter.

Thus informed by many of the world's major belief systems, and by many, many peoples' experiences (like my own), I'm going to go out on my own personal limb here and assert that there definitely *is* a Life after death. You can count on it.

When one great religion and a couple of million people say something is so, you may want to be a little wary of making any snap decisions about it. But if numerous great religions and billions of people say it's so, it may just merit serious consideration. Or if, as in my case, you've actually seen your dead body lying *down there* (as so many people have) and you were twenty feet *above* it feeling great, it may start to seem more as if it's *this* life that's being invented.

Here comes my simplified version of the basic ideas behind reincarnation.

This life of ours is part of a vast continuum of Being. Our spirits occupy these bodies as vessels until the vessel wears out—like climbing out of a broken-down car and climbing into a new one. I'm only in this particular, rather limited body for now, and it's always changing. When we leave these bodies, the experience seems to be one of liberation, of ease, and of an expansion of sorts.

So there's quite a good chance that we've always been part of this limitless underlying system, as it were, cycling through these limited physical experiences—always busily making up for the past, filling in things we've missed, and preparing our road ahead, mostly without even knowing what we're doing or why. I think that even people who claim they don't believe in this at some level really do believe in it. We all experience cause and effect in our lives—the idea that "we reap what we sow"—and it does help explain all the good and bad "random" breaks we experience throughout our lives.

Ideally, we'd come back as *bodhisattvas*, which in Buddhism is a fully aware spirit who's consciously reborn to help other people reach their own completion, to improve the expression and evolution of all. They've *made it*. They'll never have to repeat the hardest lessons again, yet they choose to come back and help others reach the point where they never have to repeat them again either. They have reached, and then help others to reach, the eventual blissful belonging-to that is everyone's birthright—after we've lived and "died" enough to have learned everything that we needed to learn, that is.

So without mincing words worse than I will anyway, here's what I believe all of this means.

If you spend, or have spent, your life in largely material pursuits, gratifying your senses, lazing your days away (or working too much), exploiting people and resources, manipulating for selfish gain, seeking the limelight, or always focusing on the sensory world—in short, not developing, but diminishing, your spiritual potential—then you will be too unconsciously *attached* to the superficial, material aspects of this life that will have absolutely no value to you later, and you'll most likely have a very bad time leaving this life in a good way. You're not likely ever to gain real fulfillment from your expression (it will just ceaselessly demand more sensory gratification), or to learn the real lessons about Love and other non-material values that would allow you to evolve spiritually beyond this life and this world. You may very well get stuck riding on the "honky-tonk merry-go-round" and have a lot to make up for in successive lives.

That's the general theory in a nutshell (and I guess a few of the possible nuts I mentioned earlier).

There is another theory as well, however, that this life we're living is what the Tibetans call a *bardo*—that is, it's not its own end at all, but a place of preparation for a higher, greater reality to come. That's unfamiliar food for thought, isn't it?

I don't know if you'd have to return as a bug or some-thing, but who knows? It may be unavoidable, and it may not even be so bad being a bug. But then it sure wouldn't be as good as it could be if you'd learned to live by a few simple spiritual principles. In fact, living by those principles might ease your suffering in this life too, as painful difficul-ties tend to pile up in proportion to your material attach-ments and expectations, and to your unwillingness to look into your life more deeply.

If you're already aware, as I think most people intuitively are, that the truly important things in life are not money, fame, sex, a Lamborghini, or having a comet named after you—all of which may be nice and have their place—but instead are Love, compassion, and developing a selflessness that contributes to all Life in general, then you're well on the way to a beautiful life, and death, and life again, and death again, and so forth and so on. Living with this *com-passionate consciousness* will give you a heightened way of being *present* for Life, for others and yourself, that com-pletely transforms and beautifies every experience, every event, good and bad, start to "finish."

Then, if necessary (and it usually is)—when we're ready, and after some kind of an assessment where we hash out a few important details (in the realms the Tibetans call the *bardos)*—we enter into another life, screaming and cry-ing, in order to continue the process of spiritual evolution that leads to an apparent completion and reunion with our Source.

In two principles of my experiences of the afterlife, there was an encompassing feeling of serenity. For me, there was simply no connection to any *body* at all, or to any material aspect of life. It felt as if I'd simply slipped out of a kind of confinement. I don't remember having any sense of occupying anything, just of opening up into a comforting, expansive totality. Nothing material, nothing that felt at all complicated or built-up. Only a refreshing sensation of calm beauty and ease. So it seems to me that happiness and serenity, and the timeless values that can help us find them in our lives, may form the golden ring we can reach for on this merry-go-round of life—the ring that will give us ever-happier rides on this carousel, for as long as we want to ride . . . and for as long as it takes to prepare ourselves in the best possible way for our passage into whatever comes next.

# Wear What You've Got On— and Leave the Baggage Behind

You have probably noticed already that nobody is really such a big deal—even if they are a big deal. We all blend into a kind of beautiful mélange of appearances and experience. From top to bottom, we inhabit life at all different levels; but then we all seem to deconstruct in more or less the same way as everyone else—particularly when it comes time for us to become just another passer-by.

All through history, there have been lots and lots of very important people—all of those kings and queens and emperors. Presidents and tycoons. Famous artists and authors. An ocean of really important people. And while their impact on millions of lives can't be denied, in the long run, they've all ended up being not such a big deal after all. Just a page in another brief chapter in the very, very thick book about all the people who ever lived—and perhaps not always in a chapter about famous admirable people, but maybe instead about the notorious ones.

At the very same time those famous folks were achieving their greatest historical impact on the lives of the multitudes, there were lots of other people living what were equally important and significant, although significantly "smaller," lives on a personal level. Maybe like your ancestors, or mine. And they were pretty important to *our* history. After all, where would we be without them?

Then there are those amazing people (like Gandhi, for example) who contribute mightily to the benefit of all, who even change the course of the world so much for the better. Maybe you are (or could still be) one of them. But even after all the contributions they've made, they, like all of us, have ended up being completely overwhelmed by the sheer impetus, the sheer unimaginable vastness and volume, of Creation. They've been returned to their Source.

There are, and have been, so very many people—billions—and yet every single one is a remarkable original full of his or her own unique potential. In fact, the most special people are often the ones you hear about the least. People who end up meaning the very most to you, and to your life. People who've been quietly showing you *how to do it right* all along. We all have examples and influences like that. People who aren't famous at all, who aren't even what society would call "successful"; yet we find that they possess wonderful qualities and a type of success in Life that we would like to have too. We want to be more like them—and we can, you know. There's time in every life to quietly become very important to someone, to a community, even to the entire world on that "smaller," more personal level. That's the truly inspiring, paradoxical power of humility.

If your life has been based on being impressive—on how many people know who you are, or on how much valuable stuff you've managed to accumulate, or by how you've "won the game" somehow—then you could be in for some complications in freeing yourself up here, because you *can* take all that stuff with you, right up to the end and beyond. You may need to reassess things quickly, because there's a lot of that metaphoric baggage—a lot of delusionally "important" attachments that accompany those big ambitions through your life—and there's no check-in at the curb where we're going. You'll have to carry all that baggage by yourself, and most of it just won't seem very important anymore (if it ever was).

The heaviest attachments are the comparisons, judgments, and grudges that you may have been carrying, sometimes without even knowing it. The relationships you may have damaged. The things you feel you've left undone. Those are the bags that we continually need to be setting down, and that we especially have to empty and set aside at the end of these lives. If you've always carried around a lot of regrets and resentments, when you can finally put them down, you'll find that, in a way, you may not really have lived yet. The weight of those attitudes may actually have been limiting your perception, suppressing your senses—getting in the way of your ability to see and to feel. But thankfully, it's never too late to get out from underneath all that.

*Now* is always the best time to set all that oppressively heavy stuff down, to lose those handicaps you've been dragging around. Now is the time to engage life with a little lightness and stop being too serious about trivial things. We're always living right now, aren't we? In *this* moment. So put the big bags down, just for now, and take a load off your life. Or, as we say in Brooklyn: Fuggitaboudit.

What you really need to carry is only what you can carry most easily, most light-heartedly. So continually remind yourself to put the heavy stuff down and travel lightly. Carry along the blessings and joys of your life—the laughter, the contributions to someone else's happiness. In short, open your heart and carry joyfulness with you as much as you can, wherever (and whenever) you go—carrying it right out in front of you, if possible. No matter how giddy this may seem to you, it is not at all superficial; in fact, it will improve your life profoundly. Being superficial is worrying about how your toupée looks or whether people are noticing your authentic designer labels—none of which makes a bit of difference if it's you that's being the fake.

Humility, by its very nature, is vastly underrated as a path to a joyful and rewarding life. It's so much more graceful than trying to impress others by acquiring and holding on to adulation or material wealth. The chief requirement is only that you show up and be a good person. So, like so many other spiritual principles, humility creates no burdens whatsoever, because the improved quality of your life is based largely on giving much of it away. Giving it back. Turning it over. Setting down the weight of self-importance and releasing it completely.

Compassion, forgiveness, and generosity are more of those kinds of profoundly significant, eternally expansive principles we really want to impress upon others, and therefore on ourselves. And if you feel you haven't found enough joyfulness to carry it out in front of you yet, or if you find yourself wishing that you'd been able to bring more of it to other people, I'm about to tell you how to start catching up on that. It's very nice work, if you can get it, and you can get quite a lot of it done in a fairly short time once you get that big, beautiful ball rolling.

And, of course, we always need to be mindful of what we're carrying along with us on this flight, just in case we have to drag it along with us onto the next one. After all, there is a good possibility that we'll all have lots of very important connections to make.

# I'll Have Extra Happiness— To Go!

If true happiness is really what we want to carry with us all the time, then why is it that it seems so transitory, so hard to capture and hold on to, much less carry along with us wherever and whenever we go? It only seems to be ours for a month or a day or just a moment, and then—*poof*—we're back to being not as happy as we would like to be. Not as happy as we may have been before.

What if I told you there were some foolproof tips for getting a hold of happiness, for keeping a hold of it and even carrying it with you wherever (and whenever) you go? And these aren't just tips that work well for day-to-day living; they're also indispensable for improving any kind of life at any time. You may have noticed that it's not always easy to be happy. It can take real effort—that's why you may not have had happiness as often as you'd wished. Like continually remembering to stop and set your baggage down, it does require some diligence.

Over the next few chapters, I'll slip in my three tips for true happiness at opportune moments, starting right now with the first one, which I call *radical kindness*. This first tip also has the benefit of being the easiest and the most fun, as you can tell it might be just from the way it sounds.

I'm going to give you this tip in the form of a challenge. Give it a try for at least one full day, but preferably two full days, and see if it doesn't completely transform your perception of life, regardless of what condition you're in. If you don't see an increase in the amount of joy, ease, comfort, and "magic" you get from everyday life . . . I'll gladly come look into it myself to see what's going wrong.

Here's the challenge.

With every person you encounter—regardless of rank or station and in any and every circumstance you find yourself all day long—be absolutely as kind and loving as you can possibly be (even if you feel lousy), without being patronizing or coming off like a boob. You have to be truly sincere, not half-heartedly sort of nice—and *never* sarcastic at all. Just be kind, without forcing it or being too enthusiastic.

Everyone has a good idea of how to be sincerely kind, even if they don't have a lot of practice.

Remember, being negative in any way is never kindness, so simply don't go there at all. Resist the urge to complain about anything. No gossiping or sharing amusements at somebody else's expense; keep only the best of intentions in your heart for everyone you meet. Be as totally tolerant and forgiving as possible, even with the most awkward or abrasive attitudes you meet. Just look people in the eye, smile with your eyes first (if you know what I mean), then smile sincerely—as if you have a special secret to share. Relax, open your heart, and be really, sincerely easy and friendly to them . . . and then watch what happens.

Your world will come to life in a way you may never have experienced before, no matter what your circumstances are. Almost immediately, allies, compatriots, and new friends who feel like old friends will begin to appear everywhere—often out of nowhere. You'll find yourself getting special treatment, being let in on insider knowledge, even being handed things you need right when you need them by people you didn't even notice were there!

And everywhere you go, you'll be met with increased joy and camaraderie—sometimes when you least expect it. Beneficial synchronicities will begin to happen all over the place, as if you were being connected by a warm, invisible fabric. Suddenly, it will be as though you're living in an entirely different world. You are. You're living in a world experienced through the filter of *kindness*. And the remarkable part is how much dullness and apathy get stripped away by that filter. It's a *real*, active power—a positive Life energy that you'll realize when you apply it.

All you have to do is continuously return the favors. Be pleasant and polite; be magnanimous and generous; be tolerant and interested; be honest and sincere—and the world will activate effervescently in the most unbelievably wonderful ways. It's the single easiest and most effective way to completely transform your life for the better. Life becomes much more fun, and a whole lot easier—even, and especially, at those times when fun and ease seem most unlikely.

Then, to really enjoy your new friends and create even more happiness in your life, become a radically good listener. Teach yourself to concentrate on what the other person is saying, not on what you're thinking about it or what you want to say next. To put it very simply: Everybody loves and deserves to be heard, and will love you for listening. Our stories and songs are often the most fascinating things we possess, so that music of the human heart is endlessly enriching.

But the point isn't to get everyone to like you—that isn't really the important thing. The point is to bring more of that beneficial energy into your life, and into the world. So try it; pry open your heart and replace all judgment and comparison with kindness for just two measly days, and watch how well it works.

Good old Mahatma Gandhi certainly had it right when he said:

Be the change you want to see in the world.

Radical kindness can change the whole world because a great deal of the time, *the world is reflecting you* by what you're bringing to your perception of it. Much of it depends on how you're feeling at any given moment, so you may imagine the world as if it were plastic, forming itself to your attitudes. If you can sustain an outward attitude of sincere loving kindness, you personally come to experience a much kinder world bouncing back at you.

This doesn't mean there's no nastiness afoot. Life can be a messy, unfair business, and apparently sadness is a painful (and sometimes kind of sweet) feeling we're meant to experience over and over. Naturally, you'll go on feeling those feelings and hearing about nasty and unfair things all the time. It's just that you won't experience them with as much urgency and ownership in your personal world anymore. The energy of kindness is really that powerful, that transformational, and that protective—I guarantee it.

And if you don't think it'll work that way for you, well it'll only cost you two days of being really nice to everyone to find out.

That's my first tip for finding happiness. The rest are on their way. But, in the meantime, let's look at what underlies, at what really creates, the power and effectiveness of radical kindness.

# Love Is the Medium, the Small, and the Large

Love is the truest content, as well as the constant current and flow, of all Life and being. Thank you for coming everybody! Goodnight! Drive home safely!

When you remember all the prominent occasions of your life—the special victories, appointments, rewards, all the good times—underscoring every one of them has been the atmosphere of Love, and Love's presence within each of those moments bubbles up through every happy memory.

All the most meaningful parts of your life—often just little things like laughing with a little kid, or soaking in the blissful beauty and solitude of nature, or that unforgettable meal with those very special friends, or giving a simple gift that may have changed someone's day (or even someone's life) for the better—all these special moments have arisen out of Love. But I'm sure that all of us, in our hearts, suspected as much already.

*All* of the most difficult and damaging parts of life originate in those conditions created by the absence of Love. On the grand scale of things, without the selfish and exploitative parts of human nature that cause so many problems for our planet and its inhabitants, there would only be the beautiful supportive flow and creation of Love. If absolute Love were our primary goal and motivation, the Earth and all the people on it would be in pretty wonderful shape.

That's pretty simple and obvious, and may seem rather airy-fairy, but it really wouldn't be so bad, would it? For everyone to take care of everyone else, and the planet? In fact, I believe it's the real goal we all share in "the end"— to accompany and lovingly care for everyone, including, of course, our Mother Earth.

Here's something interestingly scientific, paraphrased from an overview of research conducted by the Institute of HeartMath, *The Science of the Heart: Exploring the Role of the Heart in Human Performance.* Did you know that medical science has now determined that the human heart, unlike any other organ in the body, contains a complex cellular structure similar to the brain? The same kind of neurons, neurotransmitters, support cells, and so forth. In fact, our hearts are directly linked to our brains, and, along with being able to learn independently, remember, feel, and sense, our hearts can enable our brains to perceive certain things, to inspire types of thoughts, and to determine our emotional experiences. And what do you suppose constitutes that energy of the heart? That forms the language of the heart? Yes, it's the *medium*—the smallest (as in humblest), as well as the overwhelmingly grandest, of Life's most visible "invisible" energies—Love.

In fact, before moving on to your next undertaking (pardon the expression), it may help you to realize that you are adrift in, surrounded by, and have always been swimming in an invisible river of this energy—this virtual ocean of Love. It's easy not to see it. We tend to keep our heads above its surface, while our hearts are submerged down in it. Even when it seems that Love is nowhere to be found, much less the principle medium of Life, if we strip away all the impositions of human will and ego, it's always right there, even in its trace forms of regret or contrition. Engaging with it is a beautiful calling.

So the main job of life is simply to eliminate the obstacles that prevent our experience of Love—the free flow of Love into us, out of us, through us, and around us. But unfortunately, it's not all that simple, is it? We need to strip down all our ideas about the world, and especially about ourselves; we need to learn to swim naked in this river of Love and become one within this medium—this subtle and beautiful energy that can carry us securely through this dimension of life, and beyond. And who among us, I ask, doesn't like to swim naked (especially in the dark)?

Put aside your reservations (and inhibitions) for a moment if you will, and let's go skinny-dipping. Here's how. Since Love is all understanding and acceptance, naturally it's what allows everything to be as beautiful as it possibly can be in our perception. When we open our hearts and accept everything and everyone as they are, simply and *without judging or comparing*—when we put a hold on every negative label or thought—we're briefly granted the ability to see Love as the medium of Life that it is shining through, as well as to witness the sometimes heart-breaking nature of life's constant struggle to return back to the source of Love.

When we open ourselves to this current of compassion that's running through Life, we can find ourselves within it and realize that we can actually *live* there. It becomes obvious that it's constantly flowing right beneath everyone and everything; and then even what seems terrible to us is exactly what it needs to be, doing what it needs to do for its own expression and evolution back toward Love—and for our return as well. Instantly, within that moment, absolute tolerance and acceptance become literally a no-brainer. We describe people who live in this flow of Life as being "all heart"—as in, "she's all heart," or "he's all heart."

If we open our hearts and use them as very nice alternative brains to process the world (instead of only using our calculating brains), we see the world through a filter of loving compassion, and instantly everything and everyone become just fine the way they are—and, in fact, as truly beautiful as Love allows them to be (sometimes a little sadly beautiful) in their own right. *All* of the pointless distinctions, all of the obstacles between us begin to dissolve into insignificance.

Each person takes on that wonderful quality of himself or herself, bumps and all. They may all be crazy, God bless 'em, but they're all beautifully, uniquely crazy. Everyone you've ever known becomes kind of perfect, even if in a very imperfect way. Everything that has ever happened or will happen in your life and in the world—even if it seems absolutely terrible—is fine as it is, because it needs to be that way in order to change and connect back to the flow of Love, back to the place where Love sympathetically carries it all—and you as well. If you just allow it to.

If you try your best to *become* Love, to personify it, you'll find you never have to worry about who you are, what you look like, what you have (or don't have), what you've done (or haven't done). You just won't need to worry about your outsides ever again. Your insides will become your outsides.

And there goes the swimsuit.

If it's still hard for you to accept the concept that Love is the true creative medium of Life, and that all "evil" and unwarranted struggle is caused by inescapably *human* attitudes and conditions, then consider that you may be suffering unconsciously from those same unfortunate human attitudes and conditions a little bit yourself. And that's what keeps you from realizing the real Love that's underneath everything. As is often the case, whatever makes you most uncomfortable in life may be what you're carrying around inside of yourself, without really seeing it. You'll need to take a really honest, objective look at what's actually blocking you from the Love. You'll usually find it pretty easily—hidden in plain sight, in fact—but only when you're being steadfastly honest with yourself.

Timeless wisdom suggests that Love and honesty are the simple keys to all human solutions. Here's the ideal formula:

Love + Honesty = All Solutions.

Let go of all those petty external details that have nothing to do with that ideal (and they all are pretty petty). Try to de-energize your internal obstacles to Love by noticing how your mind wants to label and categorize everything as "good" or "bad"; then make a concerted effort to relax and relinquish that incessant need to judge everything you see automatically. Instead, try to see it as what is *Love* and what is *Not-Love*. If it is clearly Love—jump on that bus. If it's Not-Love, then you may ask yourself this one question: Have you brought along enough extra for everybody? At these times, it may be up to you to supply what's missing.

You never need to deny or hide from the apparent antithetical "reality" that evil exists in the world. Why would you? Good illuminates bad, as day replaces night. The moon is always there, only it's the sun that brings Life. The poison of evil exists everywhere there's human willfulness and ego. But when you do your best to experience the medium of

Love and become one with it, you'll become the antidote to that poison. You'll join up with a deep, invisible river of the antidote.

I'll speak of Love as a physical *field of being* (like gravity) over and over, and because of the idyllic romanticism attached to the word, it may start sounding like so much gratuitous gushing. So please, call it whatever you want instead. Call it God. Call it Reason. Call it sanity, or compassion, or entanglement. Call it Creation, or the Universe. Because for our purposes, in my book, it's all the same.

# Time to Tie
# Your Loose Ends Up

You know in India, and especially in Tibet, they've really got all this life-and-death stuff completely figured out. They even have names and categories for everything, and there are no questions unanswered about whether or not we go on after this life—or how. It's all been clearly understood for thousands of years that we're simply part of this great cycle of Being. Our individual lives are just one little snap-shot of it. But of course, to you and me, it happens to be an important little snapshot. It's the portrait of our "entire" lives, after all.

The Tibetan Buddhists even have a multitude of poetic categories of after-life existence. Have you ever heard of a "Hungry Ghost?" One definition is that of a spirit who's left this plane of existence, but hasn't joined the flow of Being, the river of Love. Someone who keeps a hold on past-life experiences, people, and places on "this side," and so is prevented from progressing spiritually after death. People like this are still too engaged with all the material stuff here. They're ghostly vestiges stuck between worlds, forlornly searching and transparent.

Ghosts are another one of those fascinating real phenomena, like reincarnation. There have been a zillion sightings through the ages. Scores of excellent photos have been taken. Videos and audio recordings document their existence. Personal experiences and testimonials of every type have come down through time in every culture. Whether it's a mass delusion or just weird, left-over traces of humans *being,* what's the difference? It's just as haunting—especially if *you* experience it.

You've heard the apocryphal stories. Mysterious nurses save patients' lives where there are no nurses on duty. A man with a handlebar mustache shows the way to safety from an old building that's on fire, then is later recognized from a photograph that's 100 years old. Children develop tragic fatal diseases, but speak and behave like wise old souls before they pass on. A girl awakens in the middle of the night to find her grandfather in her room, offering her loving encouragement about something important that she's trying to do, but the next day she discovers that he died that night, at the very same time, many miles away.

Isn't that beautiful stuff? It's all the work of spirits who apparently have stopped back in to lend a hand. Just to make sure you turned the coffee off. "Angels." That's nice. Maybe they're part of an army of full-time angels, or maybe they're just singular souls tying up a loose end or two themselves. Even as "ghosts," they can embody Love just as we can in this life. Spirits who are painfully stuck in a limbo without Love are selfish and scary . . . and noisy. That's why all the most famous ghosts are the spooky ones. Even though there are far more kindly, angelic ghosts running around being helpful to people, they tend to go about their business quietly, with consideration for our fragile human fears.

But it's Love as *the medium* that we want to focus on, so we need to recognize it and utilize it as the means to smooth out the rough spots in our own stories.

Love, by its true nature, is light as air. So if there's anything in your life that feels heavy, it's probably an obstacle to Love—a hitch in your spiritual evolution that has to be worked out and resolved patiently and methodically. So what exactly are those hitches, those obstacles that keep us so woefully and so wrongfully stuck in the painful parts of this life, and possibly in the hereafter as well?

They are the heavy, painful attachments from which we need to free ourselves. Grudges, resentments, perceived injustices, and morbid obsessions constitute the psychic quicksand that can get us so painfully stuck living this life badly, and leaving it badly. Sticky, nasty unfinished business. It's time to neaten up those loose ends if possible. But how do you go about it?

Start by allowing that you are only a small (but quite important) part of a very large thing. Realize that Love is the true underlying medium of Life's grace. Acknowledge that people are all subject to their origins and all the ups and downs of their own lives—just trying their best to work with what they have. When you can do this, then you're ready to become *unstuck* using a method that also happens to be my second tip for finding true happiness. This one I call *radical forgiveness* and, like radical kindness, it's also very powerful, and pretty self-explanatory as well. It goes like this.

Whenever you see someone as having injured you in any way, someone whose "unfinished business" baggage you may carry into your future; or whenever anyone does anything to you that you perceive as (or that truly is) offensive or damaging to you—from stepping on your toe to stealing your wife; from stiffing you on a payment to sticking you with the check; from "deeply disappointing" you to "ruining your life"— *forgive that person as immediately and as completely as you possibly can.* Poof! Forgiven. Just like that. It can really be that easy. Stop thinking about yourself as being at the center of everything, and put your "injuries" in perspective with all the life on the whole planet for that exact moment it takes you to forgive. And at that exact moment, *set* that change in your heart, just as if you were shutting down some noisy machine for good. That's the idea. It's like shutting down that noisy obstacle-making machine in your head.

Remember, everyone is fighting the same battles, and many people are doing it with even louder voices in their heads than you or I may have. Become grateful for that immediately, and the noise diminishes. Recognize that, when others have done something hurtful to you, it's usually a sign that they're suffering themselves. They have to listen to that racket all the time—that form of self-hatred—and you just unfortunately happened to be in their line of fire at the moment.

If you stay invested in other people's pain, you'll carry it around with you as if it were really yours—when, of course, it isn't. Take the opportunity to transcend the petty destructive and unconscious things that we humans can sometimes do, usually in an effort to enhance or "protect" ourselves, and instead try to see them as opportunities to deal with someone's pain (maybe your own?) with generosity and compassion.

*Compassion* just happens to be the juice that facilitates life's natural ease and balance. And of course, compassion is Love. There it is! You've found it underneath the will and ego again, at the level of your open heart. So you can either just radically forgive people, there in your heart (that would be great), or, even better yet, let them know the next chance you get that everything has been forgiven.

You can call those you forgive, or drop a letter or e-mail; send them a little gift; include them in a social event, or a private occasion when they don't expect it. Share something with them that signals to them that Love has won out after all. That all is well between you. If you don't have that opportunity, or just can't get yourself to do it, sincerely forgive them in your heart—that's okay too.

That's my second tip for finding happiness. You see, it does take a little effort, but nothing you can't handle.

Oops! There's something important I forgot; that part about having compassion for someone else's pain (or your own) reminded me. At this point of radically forgiving, if you're really being honest about it, you just may notice that the terrible thing you may have thought someone else did to you was actually the terrible thing *you did to someone else*. I hate when that happens. Maybe that contributes to the persistence of that particular pain. So first you may want to begin the forgiving process a little differently, by radically forgiving *yourself*.

That's right. Forgive yourself completely for everything you've ever felt you got wrong. Everything you've ever regretted. As long as it's just between you and you, why not give yourself a break? Very few of us will ever approach any kind of perfection. Maybe we'll have a chance to someday, but not while we're dragging our old regrets around. Even if it's something really awful you did long ago, let go with both hands, as well as you can. We all have to deal with the consequences of our actions at some point, so go ahead and take the first step now. There's nothing that hasn't been done before, or that won't be done again. Use the acceptance you find for yourself, the acceptance of your own human weaknesses, to open up your channel to the compassion you'll use when you forgive others.

There's only one sure way to tie up the loose ends that you know are really *your* responsibility. Go ahead and take the time to write (or dictate to a confidant) a quick list and a truthful "what happened." Just making this list will open you to forgiving yourself—the self-honesty is a release in itself—but it's still best to take some action. So, as soon as you have the nerve (or before you lose it), contact the victim (or victims) of your human error. Write them a letter, or give them a surprise phone call, out of the blue. Offer them a genuine concession to grace—an olive branch of apology. If it was an injury that you honestly know was your fault, acknowledge that you know just what you did and apologize to them, right from your toes up. If there was damage done that can be repaired, and some way you can compensate for it or actually correct it, go ahead and do it.

What would be the point, at this point, of not patching things up, of not "coming clean"? You don't want to get stuck in that endless line, carrying someone else's old bags just when you're setting down your own. *Now* is always the time to repair those old injuries by using Love, some guts, and heartfelt, principled action—just like glue and spackle and a fresh coat of paint. Not like new, but *from now on*.

If others won't accept your apology, or keep holding to a pattern of confrontation, let them be who they have to be. Some people will never let go of what seems like a justified grievance. Maybe you can't blame 'em. Gently insist on an understanding resolution, and if they continue to resist, just give them your blessings and *let go*. You've done your part. From now on, it's the way you choose to live your life that will heal the past.

Somebody may have done something really awful to you in the past, or may be behaving that way now. You never have to accept that egregiously hurtful behavior completely, only to recognize it as a part of the whole, as an expression of suffering. That's what people have to express, that pain—that's why they cause injury. Some terrible trauma probably happened to them to make them that way. It's nearly always true that abusers were abused themselves. Find compassion in your heart, and radically forgive them as best as you can. Simply and gently remove yourself from it, physically and spiritually, and keep moving forward into new life, knowing that you're free of it now. Knowing that your compassion contributes to their potential healing, and to your own spiritual evolution.

The positive effects of tying up your loose ends will amaze you anytime you do it—regardless of what life schedule you're on. It's all what modern Buddhists call "burning up negative karma." That's right—*karma*: "What goes around, comes around." It actually translates as "action," and that's what tying up your loose ends is all about—taking the right actions. Smoothing out those rough spots on your path; making an effort to remove the obstacles and handicaps; letting go, opening up, and aiming for a higher trajectory from here on out.

With our loose ends tied up, we can begin making more of the good stuff we do want to take along with us. Not things, or simply good impressions, but the real karma of Love that can pave the road ahead with serenity and peace of mind.

In Tibetan Buddhist tradition, when the Dalai Lama dies, the search begins to find him again. They meditate on it for a long time, and then follow their leads to find a boy who was born at the right time. One of the tests they give the little boy is to sit him down in front of dozens of personal objects. If he picks out everything that belonged to the recently passed Dalai Lama without hesitation and with perfect accuracy, the boy is obviously the Dalai Lama returned. Right back on his very special mission as an ambassador of Love and compassion (a *bodhisattva*) to aid the spiritual evolution of the world.

You have been, and still are, on your own special road, receiving what you've needed to grow and find yourself. To evolve your spirit. If the externals have always been getting in the way, now's the time to stop allowing them to define you. Look within yourself, honestly—get *really* honest with yourself. You will know what ends need to be tied up so that, as this life declines, your spiritual life can expand unfettered—right out beyond this world and into your new life.

Remember, as in the instant that a butterfly emerges from its cocoon, the most important transformations can take place in just a moment or two. So even if that's all you seem to have left, these very important projects can still be accomplished *that* quickly in your heart. You can reach that atonement (at-one-ment) in the brief measure of a single falling tear. It only takes a moment to choose how much you want to clear. How free you want to be. It's your choice to make.

Make the time to find and fix your own karma in your heart. You'll know where all those loose ends are, and what actions you need to take to tie them up. And, if you don't release those obstacles to Love now, you'll probably end up dragging them around like the spooky old chains of the Ghost of Christmas Past.

It just takes a little time, some resolve, and a bit of courage to gain the rewards of that wholeness. To become free. And believe me . . . it's worth it.

# And Now a Few Scenes from Another Close Call

Here comes my second Near Death Experience. I hadn't intended to include it at first, because it wasn't as "impressive" as the first one. It didn't seem very meaningful to me for a long time, so I didn't think it was important enough. But then I knew that was really because of some feelings I had around it.

When I got honest with myself about it, I realized it was those feelings that caused my aversion—not that the incident wasn't meaningful. It was deeply meaningful; and since it was such a different type of experience, it's all the more important for me to tell it. It's just a little hard to do because of a certain embarrassment factor. It just doesn't make me look too good, which for me is kind of a tough nut to swallow—and more nuts is not necessarily what I need.

So, how's about if I just cut to the chase, and begin with me already lying on the floor? Would that be too obviously elusive of me? You see, the circumstances leading up to the event weren't particularly pretty. That's why I always hesitate to revisit it. It is the unattractiveness of the situation that makes it seem foolish and unimportant by comparison, though I suppose it's something significant in itself when one of your Near Death Experiences doesn't seem to measure up to another. However, it's too important and too instructive to leave out, so here it is . . .

Let's just say that the situation came about as a result of my burning the candle at both ends again—only this was some years later, and it was more like a Roman candle, if you get my drift. And I was truly drifting at that point in my life. I couldn't figure out who I was or where I was going, despite having more professional success at the time than I'd ever had before.

I was lying on my back on the wooden floor of my big city apartment, with my head propped up against the exposed brick wall. I'd barely made it home from an occasion my girlfriend had been aching to attend for weeks. She was hoping the evening would be something unique and exciting, and I guess it was, but not for the reasons she'd thought. She'd been right about the party—it was exciting and dangerous, with a wickedness creeping in from the edges. Wild, "fun," provocative things were happening—but I, most definitely, was not.

At a certain point early in the party, I suddenly began to feel all the blood draining out of my head. Something very bad was happening to me, but I had no idea exactly what. It could have been a lot of different things, and probably was all of them. I knew I had to get out of there, to get home as quickly as possible, if at all possible. Our apartment was only a block or two away, but it seemed like miles in the failing light of my cascading physiological shut-down.

My girlfriend wasn't happy about having to leave her party, and told me so all the way home. And now she stood over me, backlit in the darkened room, enthusiastically voicing her disappointment. But I really couldn't hear a word. Her voice had receded almost entirely, as the whole room had, behind a dense misty veil of sorts. The dark room had filled in toward me with a bright white fog, as if I were surrounded by the inside of a cloud. I blinked, staring into it, and blinked hard again; but a profoundly brilliant whiteness was all I could see.

Physically, I had no sensation. I felt as if I had no pulse from the inside out; there was just no tension of any sort in my body. All my physical systems seemed to have stopped. I didn't feel at all disembodied; I just couldn't move.

Then something started up—something otherworldly—and someone began speaking to me softly: "Look here . . ." A sort of screen surfaced from out of the white vapor—like a window or a TV screen—and a scene appeared. I can't remember now exactly what the scene was, but I recognized it immediately as being an important moment from my life—one I hadn't thought of for quite a while. Not a "greatest hit" type of memory at all—much more critical in a way. A turning point. I remembered it like one of those important parts of a dream you tell yourself you won't forget when you wake up, but then you do. Then the "screen" changed, and showed me yet another elusive, important moment, and I was watching, and living *that* again.

It was as if I were being asked to review these moments, these pivotal, forgotten moments. And I remember thinking: My God, this *actually happens*, your life "passes before your eyes." Only it wasn't the life I would have expected. It was this selection of honestly significant moments that I probably should have learned something from, but apparently hadn't—although I felt no pressure, no judgment, no blame about anything. I didn't really feel anything at all, except for a dreamy, comfortable softness and ease. It didn't occur to me that I might be dying. I was just resolutely paralyzed, interested, confused. And kind of content and happier than I'd felt for a long while, in an odd, terribly injured way.

At that point, I began to hear a regular voice again: "You're not doing that!" It was my girlfriend. "You are not going to do *that!*" I remember thinking that, if "that" *was* dying, then what would she do to me if I did? I'd be dead already. Then, in a meek, worried tone, she said: "Do I have to call somebody?" And her suffering reached me. Life began slowly pouring back in. The scenes faded and, as the enveloping white mist receded, her face, rather close to mine, rose back to the surface and filled my vision from top to bottom. Color thickened in the room. The light got dark and hard behind her again. Then the world felt hard again as well.

It took me quite a while even to sit up, and quite a bit longer to stand. I recovered more or less completely, but only physically speaking. Within a couple of weeks, I'd announced to her that everything in my life had to change. I broke up with her, gave up the apartment, and moved clear across the country from the East Coast back "home." Back to the lonesome, dusty ocean of the desert Wild West.

Of course, wherever I went, I took my self along.

What did I learn from all that? Not much at the time, I'm afraid, but like my earlier near-death incident, the deepest meanings of the experience sank in much later; or actually, they arose from deep within—but only when I was finally ready for it all to surface again. In fact, it wasn't until fairly recently that I had the willingness to go back there, back into it. Then I finally began to realize what it all meant, and how it fit into my life—or more accurately, how *my life* fits into *it*.

So, is it some kind of amazing biochemical shutdown syndrome that's made the concept of "your life flashing before your eyes" such a cliché with people who experience near death; or is it an actual witnessing, a review of the "Akashic Record" (the heavenly book of our lives)? An overview of your rough spots? The state of your spiritual evolution? The unmet requirements you definitely still have to deal with? All taking place in a dimension alongside or beyond this one, that is.

I can't tell you which it is for sure, but I can tell you that it did feel a whole lot *like school* (as my first NDE had a bit); and it seemed as if I would definitely be reviewing all of this material later, and even that there might be a test of sorts involved. It dawned on me how profoundly important it was—that there does seem to be a record of it all, an account of the incidents that have formed our lives. And just as our past lives influence our current lives, our entire lives to this point influence where and how we will move on from this part to the next.

Slowly, I realized that every moment in my life most likely matters a lot more than I had ever considered it did before. That I'm never simply alone and adrift, but instead connected to a profound, invisible system. That having real presence and positive *character,* and taking right actions, can create a more deeply satisfying life, and apparently is the real mechanism of our evolutionary progress.

Of course, I'd had those cursory lessons about good citizenship that we all get in school, but they had never really sunk in like that before. I still didn't do much about any of it for a long time afterward, but eventually it began to resonate within me, to percolate quietly. Up until then, the only "real character" I was acquainted with was a person. Character as a quality was clearly a good thing to have, but it was still somewhat theoretical to me. Behaving with true character requires a real effort which it had never occurred to me that I needed to be willing to make. I thought I was okay without trying, just floating along. I'd never thought much about the world outside myself, about my place in a much greater order of things—and that it might take some work to play my true part in it.

But finally, the experience helped me to change; it also gave me the chance to come back from that particular edge and describe to you the same scene that so many "near-death" survivors have described before me—the part where you review your life as it passes before your eyes. The part where you see yourself as being truly responsible for the defining moments of your life, moment by precious moment. Even when they don't seem so momentous at the time, *they just may be.*

I believe that we do go back to school in a way, based on our past actions and deeds in this life, to inform ourselves and our futures at a spiritual level; so it compels me to warn you that, if you haven't given any of this stuff much thought up to now, you may want to begin considering it more as a long-term reality.

For some lucky people—people who are much more spiritually evolved than I—I'm sure it's never an issue at all. They've naturally learned how to be present and measure out life with the appropriate balance between taking and giving. It's their karma, and their karmic actions flow naturally. They naturally receive high marks in class. That remains something to which I aspire. But nobody's perfect, and if you're anything like I was, you may want to review some of those moments from your past before your future suddenly comes barreling along like a crazy tornado.

Make an effort to really pay attention to Life, and take the extra time just to do things a little better. Then notice the results you get, and let that guide the actions you continue to take in each and every moment. Every moment *can* matter.

# The Fat Lady Never Sings—Unless You're at the Opera

You may have noticed that I've been dancing and dancing with this one wonderful partner since we came in—namely the idea that what we call dying is really just the transition that takes place when the bodies we currently inhabit wear out and our spirits exit and move on along. I'm secure in personally bearing witness to that phenomenon. I've exited my body a little, I guess, a few times. But if you haven't experienced that disembodiment that some people have, it can be pretty hard to come to terms with the idea of being two separate parts—an expansive, timeless spiritual self and a material, physical self that's got a somewhat flexible expiration date.

We experience the events of our lives—we experience *time*—simply as a function of our bodies' biology, it seems. The more important it is to us how our bodies look and feel and work, the more anxiety we tend to experience with the passing of time. Naturally, how we look and feel is important, but when we overly identify our sense of self with the appearances and functions of this body, we can make all our inevitable changes and life transitions more complicated or difficult, or both. It doesn't matter whether the appearances and functions I'm talking about are the very pleasant and gratifying ones, or not-so-pleasant and plainly embarrassing. It goes back to the idea that the more *self*-centered we are, the less we flow within the sustaining medium of Love, and the less comfortable we feel.

If we hold on to the enhancement of our physical being as the focus of our lives, we tend to feel as if we're somehow never enough (especially as we get older). But if we keep Love as the focus of our lives now (and it's always *now)*, it won't really matter nearly as much what stage we occupy in our chronological "body-life."

I've been talking about "Life after life," about reincarnation and karma and all, as if I just expect you to buy right into it. But it does require something like a giant leap of faith for those of you who haven't experienced any profound glimpses behind the curtain, so to speak. So how about a not-so-profound glimpse? A lengthy peek we all get on a daily basis, our whole lives long.

Every night when we sleep, we're experiencing a little bit of what dying was like to me. Our present bodies are not really in the picture, at least not so as to notice them much. This doesn't mean we aren't ourselves, whoever the heck that may actually be, when we're asleep. The main sensation for most of us in "dreamland" is that we're pretty detached, and subject to whatever we may find there, or whatever may find us. But then, sometimes all life seems to be a bit that way, doesn't it?

Strange and funny things do happen in our sleeping dreams, however—and not necessarily "ha-ha" funny. We've all had weird dreams—some very disturbing, others fantastically beautiful. Or we may experience deep dreamless sleep, but when we awaken we're right back in the same place—proof of a kind that our deeper selves exist independent of our waking lives, with or without the sense of control that this waking consciousness seems to give us.

The presence that I had in my experiences of "dying" wasn't like either that I find in these states of sleep. Not the nothingness of dreamless sleep, because I was definitely *awake*; and not as crazy or uncontrolled as my dreams often can be. In fact, nothing "in death" seemed really crazy or random at all. As unusual and even dreamlike as it may have been, it all felt totally under control and actually had a kind of enhanced sanity—even beyond that of "real life." Definitely ethereal, like a dream, but completely without any dreamlike craziness.

Many of us have experienced at least some degree of unconsciousness, whether we got "knocked out" accidentally, had some surgery, or perhaps had our wisdom teeth yanked out under anesthesia. Where did we go then?

Did you know that so many people have accurately reported the details of their experiences while they were deeply unconscious or even "dying" in hospital operating rooms (usually about "floating" up by the ceiling as I did) that, in some hospitals, they've actually put symbols or numbers on top of the tall cabinets in case their patients can see them while they are not in their bodies? People have been able to report accurately on what they have seen up there, even though it was never visible from where they were lying and while they were completely "out"—as in *out of their bodies.*

Isn't it amazing that, although awareness of these phenomena exists to the degree that it should be the subject of ongoing studies, none of it has been very well publicized? It's as if it suggests something that's scary, when it doesn't. On the contrary, it suggests something very beautiful, and very important.

And who were you ten years ago? Or twenty? Have you ever been exactly the same person that you are now? There are only interior traces of the child you once were. The teen, the young adult—they've both "passed on" into memory. All of us live and die many different lives within this one. I am never quite the same as I have been—except in that one eternal *me* that I have always been at this moment.

That's a big part of our job here—seeing what it is that changes, and what it is that always stays the same. *Recognizing the eternal within each other,* as well as within ourselves. To look beyond the surface considerations, the ego's comparisons and judgments, to the true self, the spirit inside. Then, when you look at others, you'll see someone who's very much like yourself, who shares many of your exact thoughts and feelings. Someone whose light perhaps shines so brightly that you want to be part of it; or someone whose pain is something you understand so completely that you just want to help ease it. It's in that place where we completely transcend superficial attitudes that we're able to be really present for each other.

So try not to think of yourself at all as your material self: the five-foot-eight accountant with a Mercedes, or the old guy with a small pension, or the tall blond with great hair and a nice house. Just don't worry so much about your "externals"—as long as you don't offend your whole neighborhood.

A funny thing happened to me after the power of my Near Death Experiences finally settled in me: I stopped caring so much about how I look. Don't get me wrong—I try to be neat. I do bathe on occasion, and I like to think I dress reasonably well, though I guess that's a matter of taste. But take my word for it, the externals aren't improved through vanity; and, oddly enough, people commented on how much better I looked after I stopped caring so much. I believe that you become more attractive when you stop worrying about it. It isn't just skin-deep.

What does matter is that you know yourself to be the private, internal *you* that is part of everything, has come from everything, and is returning back to everything in your unique way. And in this unique way, you are just like everyone else, and everyone else is just like you.

We usually have no problem accepting the idea of a great Cycle of Life as it applies to animals and trees and plants and all of nature, because we don't share our troublesome human egos with them, only the consciousness of this Earth that conditions and energizes all of Life as we know it. When we lose the peculiar constraints of our egos, those collective and personal obstacles to Love, we become simple and free—much more like our animal partners. And even more like the flowers and trees. We become what we really are: a simple, integrated part of this eternally beautiful mystery, riding happily along on our collective cycle of life.

As we begin to identify our selves with that *eternal* inner quality, that undeniable connection, our small but necessary part in the great order of things becomes much clearer, and all of our important entrances and exits occur much more gracefully, and in perfect time with the music that is Life.

Although we will go on after this, it is very possible that this may be the only place where we'll have these particularly human, uniquely sensory, experiences. So it's important to dance, to grieve—to be *alive*. To eat together, to cry together, to have fun with one another, and to appreciate the special occasion that life on this unique planet, in this amazing body, really is.

So you see, the music will always be there, waiting for us to listen and to play along with it. But unless you've requested that a loved one actually play a recording of your favorite aria at your passing, the Fat Lady really *never* sings. But she *is* a marvelous dancer.

# Fear Is Funny—
# Ask a Bear, a Crocodile,
# or the Elephant in the Room

I talked a little about "scary" stuff back at the beginning of this book, and that darned elephant is no doubt still in the room with us. Did you happen to notice that huge, quivering pink creature in the corner? It's just our old companion, *fear*.

Fear is like a bad relation who shows up uninvited and moves in with you for an unspecified length of stay. Or just comes walking out of the guest room unexpectedly one morning, scratching his heinie and asking what's for breakfast. You don't want to have to feed him, but it's always hard not to when he moves in like that. After all, it's only the human thing to do.

If I knew how much time I'd spent in my life fearing things that never happened, I would be stunned, I'm sure. It would be one of those statistics like how much time I've spent stuck in traffic, or what percentage of my life I've slept in total.

At this point, I've probably spent years fearfully worrying about one thing or another. Yet, when I think back on it, a good 98 percent of what I was worried about never came to pass. And if the other 2 percent did come to pass, it just kept right on passing without too much consequence—or even left me better off than before.

Sometimes, my fears were answered (especially if I was helping them along, as usual) or small fears came out of nowhere and suddenly became unjustifiably huge and seemingly insurmountable. But then even those dark, looming threats turned into something self-imposed and imaginary—not based on anything real. Fear certainly can feel plenty real, however, especially when a fearful situation appears on the horizon ahead, or suddenly and unexpectedly seizes you by the neck.

Still, the one thing that has remained true at the end of all those fears is this: At least now—in this moment—I am still here (as well as can be expected) and things are okay. So I know those fears weren't as real as I am. And if you're with me now, reading this book, you are more real than those fears as well. Yet, even with this understanding, this wisdom of everything's being just the way it's supposed to be, it's still very difficult not to let fear rent space in my head.

It seems to be even tougher to accept that fear has almost always been good for me, because it's forced me to take some action that I'd been needing to take for some time. That's actually been the most real aspect of fear in my life. Then, simply recognizing the actions that I needed to take helped deflate the fear, and actually taking those actions gave me relief and renewal, and often took me to a new level of consciousness that I had never expected to find in such a "dark" place.

I imagine I would've been afraid of my Near Death Experiences if I'd known they were coming. But I didn't. Unless we're very old, or very ill, or find ourselves in a very dangerous place, I don't think we ever see a chance of it coming. In any case, it *never* serves us to make up scary scenarios about death. Instead, you might try inventing something based on my testimony, as long as we're making things up. Like there's a good chance you may not even know when death is happening, or feel it much when it does; or that it may come quickly, as a pleasant, or even *amazing* thing. So, as usual, much of that preliminary fear is not necessary at all.

Occasionally, however, fear really *is* necessary—especially if you're being chased by a bear or, God forbid, by a crocodile. I hate that. Now that's *real* fear. But if there isn't a bear chasing you, then what you really fear when it comes to death is probably just the "Great Unknown," and that's understandable too.

What has always been the biggest question when it comes to accepting an unknown? Will it be good or will it be bad—right? Am I going to be better off after this or not? I've got a very simple answer when it comes to this one particular unknown: From my personal experience, you have nothing at all to fear, except the harsh, but temporary, discomfort we may all have to expect in such a case. In the larger context, your outlook is excellent. If you're in the midst of unpleasantness and pain, the moment immediately after your transition, you will instantaneously feel great—completely free of any of the painful physical circumstances that led up to that moment. And, on top of that, if your spiritual condition is already good here, everything will be downright delightful "there." If it isn't, you'll have a chance to improve it, since that is always the nature of the process. So the answer to your big question about whether you'll be better off after this is: *Yes, you will.*

Of course, I can only speak from my personal experience. But keep in mind that thousands and thousands of people have gone on the record on this matter, and have reported incredibly wonderful things after their transitions. In fact, more often than not, they have reported ecstatic releases, joyful reunions, and transcendent surroundings. They have reported experiences of a miraculous nature.

Yet there are some rather bad reports as well. For example, my third experience was much darker than my first or my second. But I believe that was because I'd become more and more blocked from Love in my life, and was carrying almost nothing but self-centered fear. In one way or another, I believe that's the case with anyone who has a dark, or in some way hellish, transition. My experience didn't last long enough for me to delve deeper into that darkness, thank God; but I do understand a little something about Hell, having definitely touched on a bit of it myself.

If you're living in the kind of self-centered fear in this life that I was, without Love in your heart, you're probably living in a kind of hell already. Hell, as compared to how nice life can be. Heaven is an open-hearted world full of Love and light; Hell is a self-centered world without it. It is *always* so.

The long-time Spiritualists who've made it their business to learn as much as possible about *after life*, and the Tibetans that I mentioned earlier who possess that great ancient wisdom about all the various possible existences after this life, have similar things to say about this earthly life. There are a lot of great and beautiful things about it, as we all know and love, but it ain't exactly easy for anyone. And nobody comes out of it "alive"—that is, not in this old body. How well we deal with it all and move on through it depends on recognizing what our right size is in life—releasing our destructive attachments, removing the obstacles we find between us and Love, and applying all the timeless values and principles that we've had the chance to learn along the way. Things like compassion, responsibility, kindness, generosity, humor, grace, moderation, tolerance, acceptance, faith, and all the rest of that perennially good stuff.

Now let's go back to that elephant standing over there in the corner, and the world he comes from, for a real expert's assistance. Elephants, in one form or another, have lived and died on this planet for a very, very long time. In close and finely articulated communication with their families and herd members, and beset by life's challenges, they all ultimately surrender their lives gracefully, in a place of honor recognized by their kind—an "elephant graveyard." It's easy for them (and for us) to recognize that only vestiges of those elephant spirits remain where their bones rest. The elephants know that their spirits have naturally returned to the Source. They are very intelligent animals, and very, very soulful.

It rarely occurs to us, that ease of "animal being," until we unexpectedly share a sunlit meadow with a doe and her fawn, or meet a heron fishing in the same spot across the river from us, or depend on the beautiful animal beneath us when we go for a horseback ride. Our animal relatives, with whom we share this world of consciousness, come and go with grace and dignity, and automatic connectedness. When we allow ourselves less self-importance, we suddenly know in our hearts that our animal partners are much closer to us in terms of their living conscious experience than our human egos will usually allow us to imagine.

Many of us only discover the underlying medium of Love at work in the world through our pets, whose karma is to help teach us, not only this simple truth of Life—this connection to the divine—but also about how we can make our transitions naturally and comfortably. Life is always good, as long as we eat and sleep and are together, with the sun on our faces and a little cuddling. Changes come and go and rarely require a great deal of effort. There's seldom a real need for fear.

The animals go through the same instinctive, challenging struggle to survive of course; but more important, they know the graceful surrender and return to Source that's accomplished with such ease of *being* and *not-being,* which they don't just manage at their transition, but really all the time.

So calm your fears; it's all only about *changing.* Animals (like us) will never "not be." Their spirits will go on and on, and they can go on living in our hearts as well, beyond these wild, earthly realms. Every cat and dog and rabbit, and every pet you ever had. Every elephant and bear (and I guess crocodiles, too) with their simple, spiritual connections are always alive and evolving; they can always teach you about Love. They were just lucky enough in this life to have had that simple, natural contact with our Source, unencumbered by human willfulness. It's because they were never kicked out of "the Garden," I suppose.

So, it's not expected that you'll necessarily go "gently into that good night." You may justifiably have to struggle a little bit. Fear can cause that. Pain can too. But when you go, try your best to go like a lark, or a poodle, or a porpoise. . .or like that big, beautiful pink elephant in the corner would.

Now you can tell him to stop that quivering and pull up a chair. But wait . . . *not that one!*

# It Hurts When I Do *This*

It hurts me to say that I think I need to talk about pain. Obviously, there is nothing really good about pain, especially when you're in it. With some of the emotional pain we go through, people may suggest that it's "good for you," that it's "really exactly what you needed." And they're probably just trying to help us out when they say that. But still, I'd really rather not have to go there, thanks anyway.

I know this life hurts us so we can learn things, so I know that some types of pain often *are* the inspiration for personal growth, but as with any type of pain that you're suffering right now, that doesn't help too much. Nothing looks much better until after all the pain is over; then it gets a lot better right away. And maybe then, in retrospect, you can see how you may have learned something really beneficial from it—but usually not until it's over. That's why they so wisely say: When you're going through Hell, *keep going*. Whoever *they* are.

I suggested something similar a little while ago when I was talking about fear. How when pain comes from fear—from simply being afraid about a new, intimidating, or threatening situation—it may just be a matter of looking at things in a different way and waiting a bit until you can recognize that it's only the fear that's painful, and that the actual situation itself isn't really all that bad. Fear that works to motivate you only seems painful because it's often pushing you to do something you don't want to have to do. That may be more like a case of hurt pride than real pain. For most of us, we usually get plenty of real pain to go around at one time or another—in moderately small doses, I hope.

Everybody experiences some pain from each of the three major pain groups: *outer pain* (physical aches and breaks, and conditions and procedures, and the dentist, and all that awful stuff); *inner pain* (romantic heartbreaks, disappointments with yourself and others, perceived betrayals and loss); and *deep-down pain* (psychic pain or even trauma that may come from an unfortunate incident or set of circumstances in your past, or by way of your genes). Deep-down pain can originate early in childhood, with some type of abuse; or it may develop later—on a dangerous job, or by being sent off to war, or by living through a natural disaster or surviving a criminal attack, or by succumbing to some innate form of self-destructiveness like alcohol or substance abuse. So many kinds of criss-crossing pain, and so few good ways to avoid them.

It shouldn't hurt too much to take a look at the different types of pain (as I classify them) in reverse order—from the sort that sticks with you from life to life, to the kind that can just make life feel really uncomfortable right now. (Pain caused by loss is the hardest to cope with in many ways, so there's a whole chapter about that later.)

Psychic pain can be the most insidiously debilitating throughout a lifetime (or lifetimes), because the cause of it can long since be over while its effects can still sneak up on us, sometimes totally unconsciously, and undermine absolutely everything we care about and everything important to us. It can jump up suddenly and create obstacles that prevent us from being able to take advantage of our possibilities and potential. Or it can lurk just under the surface of consciousness, like a crocodile, in the form of subtly (or not so subtly) destructive attitudes that can sabotage our ability truly to appreciate Life. Our ability really to be present and live well.

Pyschic pain is also what we may refer to as *spiritual* pain—pain that affects our lives in a more profound and crippling way than a simple broken heart or personal disappointment can. So this kind of pain can also be understood as *karmic*—the product of some deep cause and effect, and something that has to be cleared up in order for us to move on effectively. It has the quality of a test that needs to be passed, or a vexing puzzle that must be solved in order to proceed freely to your next level with a feeling of wholeness and restored purpose.

The short solution to psychic pain is this: *You must find some Love to treat it with*—because you will have to have that. From there, it can be a fairly lengthy process that involves five steps: honesty, awareness, education, forgiveness, and practice. You must first acknowledge the source of the pain (honesty). Then you must investigate it (awareness) and learn about what its effects and symptoms are and have been for you (education). Finally, you'll need to reach an understanding and acceptance of what the pain's role is and has been in your life (forgiveness), and enjoy living without it (practice)!

That's generally the way you can recover, learn how to manage what's left of the pain, and put it behind you as well as possible. Sometimes it is a bit of a hike from here to there, and it's a trip that you should never want to take alone. It's practically mandatory to find a qualified guide, a spiritual sherpa, because knowing how to get yourself up and out of that swamp can require a very experienced layperson's—or possibly even a professional's—help. Here's an armchair version of the process as given by a wonderfully wise "layperson" more than 2000 years ago:

> If you bring forth that which is within you, what you bring forth will save you. If you do not bring forth what is within you, what you do not bring forth will destroy you.
> Yeshua, Logion 70, *Gospel of Thomas*

Through any healing process, it's always necessary to get some Love from other people who have gone through the same thing. You can find professionals, peers, and support groups for all the deep-down psychic pain-causing problems that Life can dish out. And when you reach out to the appropriate community of people, you'll find the necessary identification, understanding, and Love there, as well as some indispensable tools to help you repair and maintain a life as free from that particular cause of pain as possible—and maybe some others while you're at it.

Listen: There isn't anything that can happen to you that hasn't happened to someone else. When you find that someone else who can help you learn to put a painful experience behind you, then when yet another person comes along with the same problem and needs help, *you* can be that person's "someone else." *You'll* have the Love and experience needed to help them learn to deal with it, and the healing circle will come all the way back around. That's how it works, as a circle. It hurts; you get help; you learn to deal with it; you help someone else. That wheel helps you roll much more easily along any road you'll travel in Life, as Love will "make the road home *become home.*"

If you've never experienced the deep-down psychic pain I've been talking about, congratulations! You can skip that whole last part. But here's a part I bet no one gets to skip—those inner pains I mentioned, like heartbreak. Ahh, how to ease the pain of heartbreak? Boy, if I could bottle that, it would be better than barbeque sauce. I'd become a world-famous love doctor, especially because you wouldn't even need a prescription for the cure. It's just a simple, over-the-counter mixture of ingredients available to anyone, made up of:

1. Time, which slowly and effectively carries away the immediate hurt;

2. Understanding that it was all in the cause of Love, which is always the most beautiful thing to have tried your best at;

3. Keeping an open heart, because you never know what truly wonderful thing this passage was preparing you for;

4. Radical forgiveness—and remember that you must try your best to forgive the other person *and* yourself.

Radical kindness works very well to ease the pain of heartbreak too, because it puts you right back into the flow of Love. And when you're in that flow, you will not stay completely alone for long.

When others cause you the pain of perceived betrayal or abandonment, it's good to remember that when it seems that someone has hurt you emotionally, it's become *your* problem, not theirs. They've gone on to live with their karma and, until you find acceptance and bring in some radical forgiveness, you're the one who is stuck. No forward movement. As counterintuitive as it may sound—since, after all, someone "done you wrong"—the pain you experience in these situations is often a form of selfishness. Not that it's your fault at all; but if you honestly search down in your heart, you may very well have known that you were heading for a fall, that you were playing a part in the whole scenario. Life can be a little Shakespearean that way. There's also something about the crazy human ego that can make us feel as if we must participate in this kind of pain longer than necessary—as if it's somehow protecting us, when actually it's holding us back from Life.

Most of our favorite people are the ones who do just what they say they'll do when they say they are going to do it—at the greatest benefit to us and right when we think we need it the most. So naturally, we're going to suffer from expecting too much of anyone who can't live up to those rather high standards. That's the kind of subtle selfishness I'm talking about. The more we make it all about *ourselves,* the more it hurts—especially when we should have known better.

How can you cure the pain caused by being disappointed with yourself? Get over it by realizing that you're only human and, as such, it's your nature to regret what you might have done better. No one is perfect. No one's going to be a genius or a movie star or a millionaire *all* the time. Not even geniuses or movie stars or millionaires. The story goes that once, as Cary Grant was talking about his deepest insecurities, the fellow he was talking to said: "But you don't have to worry about that; you're Cary Grant!" To which the rich, handsome actor replied: "I wish I were." A story like that can give us a little compassion for ourselves, and a little gratitude for the sweetness and simplicity of our own lives. It isn't easy for anyone. We're all in this together.

There's always tomorrow. Clichés like these and many others exist solely to point out the folly of our selfish pains.

It's also why radical forgiveness is our second tip for happiness, and why radical kindness is the first. Because, if selfish pain is caused by feeling as if the Universe hasn't been fair to you—hasn't given you what you wanted, what you "needed"—then the most counterintuitive, but effective, cure to that is to summon up all your available kindness and *give something back*. Even if you feel as if you've got nothing in the bank. You do. You can coach Little League, volunteer at a shelter, make potato salad for a picnic, read to a person in a convalescent home, and so on. May not sound like much; but it is. You'll be amazed at what being helpful to others will do for you—and at the kinds of people you meet while you're doing a good deed. The kinds of people that can give you faith in humanity, as well as an indispensable lesson in the healing power of compassion.

> Heaven arms with Compassion those whom it would not see destroyed.
>
> *Tao te Ch'ing,* 67

With all these types of inner pain, most of the suffering is really caused by having to think about it all the time. Those damn "thought loops" repeating the whole miserable story over and over, and all the complications that a fearful, overactive imagination can create. We know that if we just stop thinking about it, we'll feel a lot better; and when we do, we do. We don't really have to think about it. It's just a naturally occurring obsession sometimes, but it can end up being the kind of obsession that can weigh us down calamitously. That's a good time to try a little meditation or contemplation (see the chapter titled *You Can Get Away with It (If It's an Inside Job)* to smooth out that mess in your head. Most of the time, your actual circumstances are no better, or no worse, than they were a little while before. You just have inner pain caused by the way you're thinking about them. Useless baggage you're still dragging around.

At these times, when we stand back and look at life from a little different angle, it makes sense that we're constantly *projecting* our own difficulties *onto* Life. Life's fine as it is; we're just choosing to experience it as something bad. If you're feeling badly, instead of stubbornly projecting bad feeling onto what could be a perfectly fine life, just try feeling better! Try to project good feelings onto Life like a beam of light from a spotlight, as you can by practicing radical kindness.

Before I get into physical pain—the most difficult type of pain, the kind that no one in their right mind chooses—I want to bring it all back into the context of what I learned from my Near Death Experiences. To do that, I'll need to have another dance with that eternally beautiful, plus-sized lady again.

If you think about it a little, when we say "we're only human," what we're really saying is that we are distinctly limited to what happens to us as a result of our physically *being a human.* There's a lot of physics and chemistry involved in all those aches, complications, requirements, and shortcomings. What's happening to us, and how we feel about it, is simply a function of what this form allows us. All our typical reactions and responses (and regrets)—the choices we have (or sometimes don't have)—are just what we get with flesh and blood and brain power. Hurting hurts. Feeling good feels great. It's all going to happen, like it or not.

Pleasure and pain are always coming and going, fluctuating to and fro, sometimes only five minutes apart, doing "their thing" to this flesh-and-bone vehicle, inspiring all kinds of crazy thoughts in our thinking organ—*the brain.* In a spiritual sense, we can live in a very different world from that one, but when we attach our overall sense of well-being to all the form-related, material stuff that's always changing in our earthly world, it makes us crazy. Because over the long haul, all the form-related, material stuff is always wearing out or somehow heading off into the sunset right when we thought we needed it the most.

If I know that I'm a spiritual being having a physical experience, and there are these solid, eternal, unchanging aspects of Life just beneath the surface—values, ethics, and behaviors I can choose for myself that foster Love and happiness and success—then why the heck don't I just choose them? I can't always select exactly what Life's going to give me, but I can have a say in how I'm going to handle it. So, how about if I just make it my intention to handle difficult experiences well, using some solid, dependable spiritual tools. That way, Life never happens to you; it always happens *for you,* because you can always deal with it and learn from it.

It's a much taller order when it comes to physical pain. Those other kinds of pain come from focusing on what we *don't* have. That's hard to do with physical pain, when we undeniably *do* have it. Many of us aren't as afraid of death itself as we understandably are of the physical pain that can often accompany it. We intuitively know that death will be a relief from that pain; but in the meantime, who wants to go through it? It's very disagreeable. I shudder every time I think of broken bones or surgery or crocodiles. I cross the street when I see a "skinhead"—and I'll tell you that story a little later!

I've heard people, usually athletes of one kind or another, say that "you have to go *into the pain* to work *through it.*" I think that sounds a little bit crazy. Personally, I seldom want to do either. But I guess I can see what they're talking about when the pain is constant and seems endless. I've experienced enough of that kind of pain to know. I think most of us have. Sometimes, we have no choice other than to recognize it as a particularly lousy part of being alive. We're in it whether we like it or not, and we know that we have to accept it, or it hurts all the more expending the energy to fight it. If dying is on the other side of that, then naturally, we have to go through it to get relief. It's the same problem I have with anything I don't like—*acceptance* helps me suffer it a bit more lightly. So why do I naturally tend to struggle so much with simple acceptance? I should have figured that one out by now. I must kind of like struggling, I guess.

It's not possible to just *think* pain away—or is it? There've been times when my mind wandered off somewhere and I forgot that I was in pain. It seems that, if I can disengage from my material physical self, I don't need to own all my physical discomforts with quite the same severity. Pain stops when we sleep, so it must be the amount and quality of consciousness that gives it room to grow. The trick then becomes being able to change our consciousness, to change our attitudes.

It always works to think about others (in a loving way), or to think about Love (prayer, of a kind), or to have a pet show you how Love works. In fact, a cat in your lap is very nice when you're hurting. We can let that sensation of easy comfort and peaceful Love—thoughts about our loved ones, or thoughts about how funny and magical Life is—carry us off at those times that we're called upon to endure discomfort in boredom. At those times, you should definitely avoid thinking about politics, plastic packaging, lawyers, or, in my case—crocodiles.

If Life's magic seems less than believable when you're lying there in pain, think of this crazy fact: When people believe they're getting something that will make them feel better, *they are* getting something that'll make them feel better. Over and over, it has been proven that placebos really work. When we believe that we're getting a cure, healing can actually happen. In pharmaceutical testing, sugar pills often work 60 percent of the time, when the actual medication being tested works only 40 percent of the time. Either would be better than nothing, but one really *is* nothing.

And this is funny: three sugar pills work better than one; and saline injections—which likewise do "nothing"—work better than sugar pills, because they seem more "serious" (and boy, are they ever).

So I don't know—does this mean you should ask your caregivers to pull a fast one on you sometimes? Here's the real point: What could all of this possibly mean, if not that our state of mind *projects* itself upon our wellness and adds to, or takes away from, our potential for healing? It's clear that our state of mind really does determine how we feel— all the time, our whole lives long, about everything.

It's more than just a little bit difficult to marshal a positive state of mind when it comes to bearing up under physical pain, as though it were something that you're responsible for yourself, something you somehow deserve—when, of course, it really isn't. It's simply something that happens to everyone, and we have to get from one side of it to the other—however much unknown real estate we have to cover. While we are going through it, our attitudes simply aren't up to us completely; they're understandably predetermined by physical sensations. So it does take effort to stay on top of it. Otherwise, we'd all be charming and sunny all the time.

There is a quality that we are given at those times, how-ever—a very valuable attribute that doesn't come so easily to many of us, namely *humility*. The humility that comes from being really injured is a thing of great power and specific humanity. The sometimes very painful reality of our physical constraints isn't a theoretical thing anymore.

The limitations of this flesh-and-bone vehicle, and the depth of acceptance we have to come up with from within ourselves, grants us a kind of unassailable authority that comes from the experience of it. We must never exploit it to feed our egos. No "woe is me" will ever improve circumstances for anyone.

Instead, we can try to expose this beautiful inner nature of being human to others, to freely pass along an understanding that we may be paying pretty dearly for ourselves. This experience, and the compassionate surrender that it opens us to, is a gift that can serve us very well. After all, one day we may ourselves be given the opportunity to show some fragile, tentative soul—perhaps a dear friend, a parent, a child, or a sibling—just *how* to go about dying well.

Learning how to meditate (again, see the *Inside Job* chapter later) will give you a remarkably powerful avenue to relief—a way to withdraw your *self* from the greatest pains the physical world can dish out.

Sometimes, when we're suffering real inescapable physical pain, it may become absolutely necessary to surrender to the care of a qualified doctor or nurse who can help us simply to accept humane and expertly administered medication (with a "c"). It's never a good time to suffer from being too proud.

If you find yourself in that spot, be as aware as possible of the difference between enduring pain unnecessarily and losing yourself in over-medication. Work with others to find a balance that allows you to appreciate Life and those around you to the fullest. Pain management is a finely tuned science these days. Don't hesitate to use it; but beware of anybody who seems to push it too hard, or of any tendency you may have to abuse it.

And most important, if at all humanly possible, keep kindness, forgiveness, and *surrender* in your heart. *(Radical surrender* will be our last tip for happiness.) That way, you can always squeeze a little true happiness out of wherever you are, whenever you really need it. And here's something else that seems medically unlikely, but is clinically true: Being kind and doing kind things for others will reduce the physical pain you experience—even if just for the moment of that kindness.

They say that what doesn't kill you makes you stronger, but naturally I disagree. I think what *does* kill you makes you stronger. I believe that experiencing death in this life, especially if we experience it for each other with an open heart, makes us better, evolves us spiritually, and brings us closer to our Source, which is the source and power of Love.

# A Baby Boom Goes Boom!

Every generation must have more or less the same experience of life—updated to current times, that is. The basic life cycle couldn't have changed all that much, except that we generally live a lot longer now. We obviously all get born—a shared experience that I don't think anybody can remember. As little children, our brains aren't developed enough to receive all the complicated transmissions, navigate "reality," or fill up with lots of (mostly useless) "important" stuff for a while yet. I think that's why so many little kids appear to be so endearingly insane. For a little while at least, they're free of the complicated world of "who you are supposed to be." They haven't yet reached that threshold of sanity that we call being "grown-up" (which some of us never truly reach) and which always tragically tends to interrupt our ability to perceive the simplest magic of Life. That can be our critical loss of innocence, I suppose.

It isn't until you get a little older that a slightly more adult perception starts to form and you also first begin to notice the seriousness of death, perhaps with the loss of a beloved pet—a loss that never gets any easier because of the shared innocence of our animal partners. Then maybe a grandparent passes away. Sometimes there's an illness or an accident involving a young friend or acquaintance, and occasionally the loss of another person now and then throughout your life. Then your second generational wave of deaths arrives: an uncle, a friend's parent, and on into your own parents' generation. It's a far more involving wave, that one, because it sets you firmly into a middle age when you begin to lose your parents and mentors, and when you first begin to sense that "ultimate" wave that's drawing ever nearer to your own generation—and, most important, to you.

I was born at the tail end of the 20th-century post-war American "baby boom," so I'm somewhere approaching or in the middle of that second wave. The third wave, my own, is rising up on the horizon ahead——not nearly so far off as it once was. Now I sometimes remember how I experienced death during those earlier times of my life. As a child, at first it was with solemn questions like: "Why?" and "I wonder what really happens?" That was replaced by a generally similar quizzical sadness as I passed into my young adulthood. As I got older, the deaths of people I cared about seemed to be more about *me,* and my questions unconsciously changed: "Why did it have to be them?" or "What'll I do now?" Death started to be defined more by what *I* would lose.

Being "grown up," what we call adulthood, is, in many cultures (not just ours), often considered to be about becoming "a somebody" as opposed to just simply being a part of a larger group. If we consider ourselves as special "somebodies" who make things happen in the world, then it tends to feel more as if the world is making things happen *to* us. Of course, it is an exchange; we do build lives and "reap what we sow." On the other hand, the grown-up idea that I'm somebody totally separate and special may be good for the old self-esteem, but it can too easily get out of hand and become a bit grandiose given the actual scale and eternal sweep of Life. That sense of separation isn't really very realistic, you know; it can disassociate us in a self-centered way from the real value of our experiences—in our relationships with one another, and with the events of Life and death. In this ego-based way, each of us and every generation can lose its proper perspective.

I had my first NDE in my twenties, my second in my thirties, and my third in my forties. None in my fifties so far, thank you very much. So I received this crazy, painful periodic education, parts of which remained subconscious until I finally "woke up in class" as I entered into that wave of deaths that includes my generation, as I and my peers began losing the ones we love—and each other. So it's largely for those peers that I'm writing this book, even though I suggested earlier that "it's for anybody who's planning on dying someday." Of course, it's for all of you too, but it's specifically for a baby boom that's about to go *boom*—and there's always one of those around. My boom, your boom, everybody's boom boom.

When I look around, I see calm pockets of wisdom and reason concerning mortality. But I also see so many people of my generation confused and conflicted by the "meaninglessness" of death, and becoming agitated by the inevitability of their own aging and "ending." I'm sure this happens to every generation, not just mine; but this is one of the first generations in Western culture to be almost completely, artificially separated from the experience of death. There aren't too many elderly people dying in the family home anymore. We seldom witness the grim fates of millions of farm animals, or what once were the brutal necessities of hunting to kill and eat. Because of this, life and death experiences that were once appropriately acknowledged, even ritualized in earlier indigenous cultures, have now become unsettling and unnecessary expressions of a skewed mass ego, shielded by *denial* at a global level. (We really *don't need to kill* anything except plants anymore—rice will not become extinct.)

Scary advances in medical technology add to these attitudes, as this is also possibly the first generation (and one may hope the last) that actually considers plastic surgery, hormone treatments, organ cloning, cryogenics, and genetic engineering as viable alternatives to growing old gracefully and transitioning into what we're naturally supposed to become next.

In the big, beautiful never-ending picture that I feel I've been given a glimpse of, we are required to grow up and grow out spiritually *through* this life, as is obviously originally intended—not to spend our energy and human potential figuring out clever ways to prolong this particular physical experience. Extending things artificially will seldom lead to a graceful end, whether we're talking about our physical lives or a dinner party. Like everything else, it's simply over when it's over, and on we go to the next natural stage of the game.

It's not surprising, I suppose, and I don't mean to blame a whole generation for anything other than understandably succumbing to a culture in which success can be defined in such a limited way. There are plenty of confused, "successful" people surrounded by richly upholstered discontent and the best doctors that money can buy (God bless them). We have all known them (or have been them ourselves), and perhaps have been graced to realize that there is an entirely different, more fulfilling, definition of success to be discovered by identifying with our authentic selves. A success that's experienced in our hearts.

I know it's hard not to get caught up in all the cultural misdirection and just continue struggling onward, but if we can consciously grasp and assume our roles as simple spiritual passengers on this remarkable planet, we may yet realize the unimaginable potential that our shared experience holds for us. Personally, I have found that there's a real ease in it, and the sense of a kind of divine direction that comes from being a caring "responsible rider." Collectively, that direction can straighten out our lives, and maybe our world as well. Missing out on it would be a real shame, even a "sin."

Appropriately enough, the Greek word that got translated into the word "sin" in so many religious texts was *amartia,* which actually translates more like: "to miss the mark." So "to sin" simply means to miss the mark (and to miss the point) at a spiritual level. Naturally, it's those "sins," those unconscious self-centered priorities, that really do impede our present and timeless potential for growth. Avoiding these "sins" will allow us to reach our evolutionary target, so to speak, personally and collectively.

Here's a very convenient acronym that I find helps to redirect my efforts: PAGGLES. That's right, PAGGLES. Our old favorites: pride, anger, greed, gluttony, lust, envy, and sloth. If our view of Life and our motivations arise out of any of these, or anything directly related to them, we're in trouble. We know them as the seven *deadly* sins, not because they'll necessarily kill you outright (though they can), but because they can kill you spiritually—obstruct your experience of your life (and lives) and so extinguish the potential you may have.

When I mentioned the quote earlier that Life doesn't happen *to you,* it happens *for you,* I think without a doubt that the same is true for death. Death doesn't happen to you, it happens for you (unless you are eaten by a crocodile; that could not possibly be *for* you). We're all part of a much bigger set of ongoing considerations—the big picture I'm asking you to see as the context for your life.

In particular, we need to escape that one self-centered cultural definition that's leading us so far astray—that death is our obliteration. The sad, absolute cessation of Life. The final chord of a sonata that starts wonderfully well, but ends in a dirge. That idea that we only have "one go-round," "one shot at it," and then "the party's over." There's a selfishness (a "sinfulness") in that definition that prevents us from living well, from showing up for each other with the proper compassionate presence. It's a self-centeredness that insists we should be *getting something we want* out of it all and each other when, instead, we could be forming true partnerships with one another—an understanding global fellowship of shared human experience—and creating a sane stewardship of life here on Earth. When we can get ourselves over this delusional assumption of self-importance, we can create a much less "sinful," more evolutionarily responsible, way of living.

If we know we're missing the mark with the cultural definition of death—one that leads to the fear of losing what we want to hang on to and the "I've gotta get mine before it's all over" approach—then what is a more realistic definition? What's the proper direction in which to aim our lives?

Well, Shakespeare's always good for a few spiritual bull's-eyes, like this one: Death is a consummation most devoutly to be wished! So we can see death as a lifelong goal that we struggle to attain—one that we want to meet with preparation, with humility and honor, and with open-hearted promise. It is our matriculation of sorts.

Speaking from my own experience, death is an expansion into transcendent being, for crying out loud. We need to restore death to its rightful place as a sacred ritual of passage. Let's get kind of Egyptian with it again. Don't mourn me; send me off with an open heart and a song! This party is definitely not over.

It's absolutely essential that we show up for each other with this positive, life-affirming definition of death as a continuation of always being present. Contrary to what Woody Allen requested, you must *never* take a raincheck for anyone's dying. (That's the only "must" in this book.) While we supposedly have much busier lives than ever, that's just an illusion caused by technology. The really important parts of our lives are still what's really important. Put the business aside. What technology is best suited for is efficiently arranging our lives around those important people and occasions, so that we can maintain close contact with the loved ones involved in all of our momentous life events—making the appropriate reservations, booking the trip, and *being there;* contributing whatever you possibly can; showing up in a way that honors Life's real connections of the heart; bringing Love right up to the surface, front and center where it belongs. Again, it's not about *me;* it's about *we.*

Notice, when we're "coming to the end" of our time in this life with someone we love or for ourselves, just how precious and how special that remaining time suddenly is. How intensely focused our love and appreciation for each other become in those few moments that are left. We need to try to treat each other that way all the time, and grow spiritually together in that kind of Love. We need *to recognize the eternal in each other,* always. That's what's really important here; everything else is a distant second place. These may be lofty ideals, granted; but pursuing them throughout our lives is time well spent, and leads to a sense of fulfillment that can never be matched in any other way.

From the time we reach that more adult perception we start to come upon as teenagers, to the time we lay ourselves down, our essential spirit remains generally young and energetic—especially in pursuing our passion for Life. It's just our bodies that atrophy, that break down and require costly repairs—or that just quit running. Our spirits, our eternal selves, always feel youthful. They're always ready to keep growing upward and onward, and so they do. That essential part of us can only collapse under the weight of selfish self-centeredness and that oppressively off-the-mark definition of death—and the negative effect it can have on the last third of our lives—when we permit those attitudes to define us as limited.

The truth is that we always have that unflappable, limitless *hope* that comes along with youth. Just scratch the surface and, like Love, it's always there. We've also got all that blind *faith* that we hardly notice enough even to take for granted when we're young. And, although it seems somehow harder to come by as we age, there's also more evidence of that faith as we grow older. Hope and faith are real working spiritual mechanisms that are always alive, and always will be in all of our lives. And if you just add *grace* to those two, then you've got my three favorite names for girls.

In his beautiful "childhood" story *Peter Pan,* J. M. Barrie makes his eternally young hero's mortal enemy, Captain Hook, a selfish pirate whose goal is to take control of Never Never Land, enslave the indigenous people by capturing their princess, Tiger Lily, and imprison or kill Peter, his hated ever-youthful nemesis. Peter thrives on denying him his grandiose and destructive goals.

Captain Hook is the oldest primary character in the story. He is vainly obsessed with always looking good, has already learned painful lessons about misdirected will (he lost his hand in a sword fight with his magical young nemesis), and is deathly afraid of a crocodile that pursues him wherever he goes (I'm with the Captain on that). At some point in the past, the crocodile swallowed an alarm clock, so whenever he approaches, Captain Hook can hear the *tick . . . tick . . . ticking* growing louder, like a bomb set to explode— the ticking clock of time *coming to get him.* In the end, all the captives are freed, Peter stays forever young, and, naturally, Captain Hook is eaten alive by the crocodile of time, destroyer of vanity and devourer of the impermanent.

It's not a story about how men never grow up, or even just one about a child who never does. It is a story about the presence of the ever-youthful eternal spirit that is always right outside the window of "who I'm *supposed* to be"—a spirit that can teach us how to fly to an eternal realm and that loves to harass the fearful, willful, vain, exploitative "pirate" that an unconsciously ego-driven, misdefined life (and death) can turn us into if we get stuck in the amber of our cultural delusions.

Now that's a real whopper of a story for children (be they spiritual or chronological)—a story that mixes imagination with timeless experience and creates a beautiful metaphoric mythology to live, and die, by.

You know, maybe I need to take a look at this uncharacteristic dread that I have of crocodiles. After all, they are a product of nature and the great Source of all Life. Could it be that it's really only *my fear* of growing old and dying manifesting itself as an inscrutable, cold-blooded creature with a perennially opened mouth lined with rows of sharp teeth? A vicious bag of horrifying finality?

Perhaps I really need to embrace that crocodile of my fears, so to speak, in the same way I'm asking you to step forward courageously to meet death with Love. Perhaps so.

But I probably won't. I mean . . . embrace a crocodile? . . . C'mon.

Say, may I just get my entire Financial Advice section out of the way right here? If there are serious issues, financial and otherwise, that you need to think about right now, just do your best to take care of them the way you'd like to see them be, then let go. Do it all well ahead of time, if possible, and then let the Universe worry about it all. Know that everything will work out as your karma directs it, for everyone concerned. After that, it's not your problem. There's no money in Heaven, but there are people living on after you go.

So that's it for my entire Financial Advice section. My words of wisdom: Do your very best, *and let go of the results*. It's pretty ancient advice, but it still seems to work very well for just about everything in Life.

# Can a Person Get a Little Privacy Around Here?

Nope. They say that dying is the one thing we do alone. But, as is the case with living, they're wrong about that one too. It's estimated that, globally, there are two people dying every second; so even in that, we'll never be totally alone.

There are things it seems we do alone, but only at the very moment we're doing them, that is. It's like driving a car, for example. Even if we're driving by ourselves, we're never really alone. There are drivers ahead of us and behind us. The folks waiting for us to get back home from the store with the ice cream. There are mechanics and traffic cops and road crews whose jobs depend on us. There are always people interacting with us—pedestrians and people that we may never even see, and will never know. Then there's also the idea of everybody else who ever drove a car—all those millions of miles of cumulative experience that everybody has racked up with everybody else who's ever been out there "on the road."

The point is that, even though we often feel separate, independent, apart-from, of course that's not true. Our lives reach out unimaginably farther than we think they do. You have an effect on others that has ripples and ramifications, even out to the rest of the world, whether you think so or not. We *are* like the moss on a rock in that way; we never really do anything completely alone, completely unconnected. So there's a quality of *not* being alone that comes from all that. We're never just doing it for ourselves, only to fulfill our own needs, even when we're getting a massage, or watching TV, or voting, or just thinking about what to do next. We're never really *in*-dependent, we're *inter*-dependent.

If you're anything like me, on more than one occasion you may have simply wanted to turn the darned world off and actually just be truly alone for a while. I'm sure you've taken a trip where you were completely cut off from all the daily hubbub and returned feeling fully refreshed, only to be immediately overwhelmed by all the information you missed while you were away. Well, you can't make the world go away, but you can determine the real importance of all that "necessary" information by redefining it with a couple simple questions: Does it connect me to a world of insight and compassion? Or is it just stimulating or agitating me? If the answer is stimulation and agitation (often the same thing), then the more attention you give it the less good it's bound to do for you.

It's always important for your overall well-being to try to exercise some control over the energy you're being exposed to through what you're experiencing—the environment you're in, or the people you're around, or the media you engage, like music, television, and the *virtual* world. It's good to guard the health of your inner self—being a part of things, but maintaining a little vigilance.

This is always good advice, although sometimes hard to follow if you're sick in bed or otherwise unwillingly stuck in aggravating circumstances beyond your control. Then you may really require some privacy—in which case, you should insist on it from others or turn inward and seek it within yourself (as I discuss in the very next chapter).

If you're in a facility of some kind or another where you might reasonably expect to find some peace and quiet but you're not finding any, *ask for help* from the Universe—or even from a real person. You meet literally the nicest people that way. If you're having a hard time, don't be shy about letting your needs be known. Everyone knows that everyone deserves comfort in the midst of a hardship.

We also deserve to make intelligent boundaries for ourselves regarding what may seem even the least bit toxic to us—people with bad attitudes, places where nothing good is bound to happen, violence in media, and so forth. We deserve to have those boundaries respected as part of our taking part in Life. Our media is very involving and seems to supply so much of our common interests; but, in the same way that it can lift our spirits, it can also tie us to attitudes and complications that we don't actually need at all. That's why we often feel such relief when we're without it. It's always changing and becoming more complex, while the most important things— Love, compassion, kindness, generosity, laughter, and all that—remain spontaneously real and will never have to change. They are the timeless parts of Life that go on continuously.

Like gears engaging the chaotic machinery of the world, in order to avoid the grind, it's good to engage lightly and be ready to *detach ourselves* easily and joyfully whenever we feel the need to. Go ahead and be discriminating. Listen to your heart in all affairs, and have faith in what you hear. That way, we can own the space where we make our own special private arrangement with Life, and with one another.

Meanwhile, Love is clearly and constantly revealing itself to you in every form of everybody and everything you interact with. Try to be sensitive to where it obviously *is,* and where it obviously *isn't*—in the people you have in your life, in your surroundings and furnishings, in the food you eat, and even the products you buy. Everything has an effect on Life. Engage yourself in the expressions of Life that make Love evident, and try to support and celebrate responsible and spiritual causes. It will lift you personally, as well as this big boat we're all in together.

Here comes that Mahatma Gandhi line again:

Be the change that you would have in the world.

That guy was eternally ahead of his time.

While on the one hand technology is putting our privacy up for grabs, at the same time, it provides the means for expressing our private connectedness in ways that could never have been imagined. Making informed connections is as simple as figuring out how to use the latest network or application. Use technology to tailor the connections you want, or don't want, from our vast shared resource for what you feel best serves the truth in your heart. Seek content that enlightens and uplifts your spirit, if possible. Take advantage of it from your seat in a packed sports arena, or from your cabin in the woods. If you're old enough to feel a bit intimidated by technology, a brief lesson with any twenty-year-old will teach you everything you need to know about how to use it. And if you're a twenty-year-old, you already know—you can be ever more a part of the world on your own terms.

This is how the Internet and social networking relate us to that remarkable quality of never-being-aloneness. It's a spiritual networking—the confluence of our shared consciousness and the power of Love with what has become (and will become) technologically possible. As the volume of the outside world expands inside of our lives through high technology, we can avail ourselves of an even *higher technology*—the kind we find by privately growing together toward our "higher selves," each of us into one another. This is the awesome technology of the heart, where we can rediscover the power of faith. The power behind the digital world is invisible, isn't it? The power behind faith is as well. Yet, while the evidence of each is clearly seen and experienced in our lives, one is infinitely and reliably more meaningful than the other, and so it can all come together to unify us.

If you really can't avoid all that company out there (or don't want to), just *surrender* to it. Inside of each moment we share with one another burns the fire of our deepest union—the longing and the means to transcend our separation from Love, from our shared source, and from our shared destination. Really. Even the briefest passing holds this potential, this recognition of our connectedness.

Talk about being connected—our animal friends can ceaselessly provide us the perfect antidote to technological overload, wayward misanthropy, or just plain loneliness. A few moments with a dog or cat in your lap will connect you to our divine shared source of Love and serenity, and will always have a deeper, more beneficial effect than any media (or any multitude of visitors) can ever deliver. Pets are our *karmic partners,* tapped-in organic transmitters of the Divine; and they are there for us when we don't feel like having any people around. They reflect us, empathize with us, and can teach us how to be complete in Love, just through their eternal style of unconditional friendship and devotion. They are us, too.

There's another deeply thought-provoking connection that keeps us from ever being alone, but I'll touch on that when I tell you about the last time I was in Arizona . . .

# You Can Get Away with It (If It's an Inside Job)

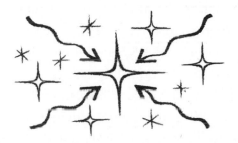

Earlier, I mentioned the fact that all kinds of discomforts disappear when we're asleep, and that changing our attitudes and thinking—our consciousness—can completely change our experience of living. That may be easier said than done; but there is a sure-fire way to make it happen. There's a place you can go where you can reconfigure your inner self, so to speak. A place where you can find as much connection, and as much peaceful serenity, as you like. A place where you can even find the means to tolerate practically anything, to celebrate even the simplest aspects of life, and to investigate its very deepest mysteries. That place is inside of you—within yourself and every one of us, in *this very moment*. It's your very own inner treatment facility for dealing with any discomfort, where you can perfect the means of becoming unflappably content. It's a kind of natural medication, only not with a "c," but with a "t" instead. It's medi-*t*ation, and it's been around a long, long time.

The great thing about meditation is that it's so practical, so easy, and so constantly, immediately available. Since it is a personal thing, it's good to practice it by yourself in a peaceful location, or along with a group of other like-minded meditators. But its benefits can be called upon at any moment—even (or especially) in the craziest, most crowded or difficult circumstances, and always with wonderful results. The difference between meditation and simply using relaxed or reverential thought to calm yourself down is that meditation is an intentional *practice*. And like anything you practice, the more you do it, the better you'll get it.

The goal of meditation—the "it" you get by practicing—is really two simple things: controlling your state of mind by controlling your thinking, and becoming aware of your real connection to Life. That's all. Pretty incredible goals to achieve while you're just sitting (or even lying) down, aren't they?

Practicing is simple; all you really need to do is relax and get comfortable (preferably in a quiet place)— anywhere and at any time. There are a few simple approaches that I've always found very helpful—and I've always needed all the help I could get, given that meditation starts us out with a rather difficult proposal, that is: What do you think about when you're not supposed to be thinking?

The first way I found is to begin by just thinking about *how* and *what* you're thinking. Listen to that subtle self-dialogue we all have going on inside our heads. Watch how your thoughts string together, and observe where they're really coming from and why—especially fears that just don't do you any good at all, or regrets that you can really just let go of at any point. *Become a witness* to the urgent, demanding voices we have coming from who knows where, and instead focus on the calm "voice of reason" that gently, constantly arises within you.

"The still, small voice," as the Quakers call it.

Sometimes, your thoughts will start going in a direction that you don't want them to go and, with a little meditative practice, you get so that you can just change them—turn them around, or even shut them off almost entirely. Thinking is just a kind of overlying process that feels as if it needs to keep moving (like a shark), but it doesn't. It actually feels a lot better to learn to slow it down, or even to keep it still sometimes. Thinking requires consciousness, but consciousness *doesn't require thinking*. It's just the action that the organ we call the brain performs, just as breathing is what the lungs are for—or like the I-have-no-idea-*what* the duodenum is for, or the appendix (there's one of those in the back of the book).

Have you ever said to yourself: "I don't even want to think about it?" Then you don't have to if you don't want to. Change the channel, as it were, to something more comfortable. To a beautiful idea or a marvelous memory. To a spectacular concept. Or simply, after a little practice, to the glow of calm silence.

The next way is to concentrate on some *experiential* or physical or even mechanical aspect of your being—like your breath, in and out, coming in, turning around, and going back out. Or like your heart beating—one, two, three, four—sending blood out to your fingers and toes, tingling, pulsing. What do you see inside your closed eyes? What the heck is going on in there? It's not nothing, is it? It's usually more like an electric dance of sorts—waves of shimmering light, fields of subtle effervescence in a darkened sea. Amazing, what all is going on inside of us.

My last best way to practice is to focus on an object of devotion. A spiritual inspiration like God, or Jesus, or Buddha, or Allah, or Krishna, or the Divine Feminine. Other inspirational figures, like Gandhi or St. Theresa. A favorite aunt who's passed away, or a loved one like your child, or your pet. Even the moon, or the oak tree in your backyard. All of these are appropriate focuses for the kind of devotional concentration that can deliver you to calm thought and a real connection with Life and with the Universe. A *mantra,* or repeated prayer or chant, can help you focus and relieve you of wandering, unnecessary thoughts. Pick one you like, and try it out.

Sometimes (lots of times), it won't be only one of these three approaches that works for you, but some combination of all three. They all work together.

Welcome to the wonderful world within, the world of meditation (with a "t"), or contemplation. Seeking the serene connection within. Exploring the rich world of divine imagination available within that expansive inner space to which we all have direct, personal access. The truly amazing thing about it is that within, "by yourself," you have the means to find all the peace you could ever want, the means to discover all the wonders of our mysterious inner universe—memory and realization. You may find new aisles and shelves in your mind's library that you've never visited before; or you may leave "the building" entirely to explore your unexplored realms of inner awareness. Really. Monks do it all the time. So do business types, artists, academicians, and even the proverbial used-car salesperson. It's free to all, and it can create profound personal freedom for everyone who gives it a little practice.

In there, in meditation, as the transient demands of unnecessary thinking begin to fade, you'll find the path to compassion and forgiveness that will improve even any of life's "most dire" situations. You'll find that many tough situations are of your own making, and not really such a big deal in the Great Scheme of Things. Along with watching your thoughts string together—which can relieve you of the nasty, fearful self-dialogues from which you may suffer— you can focus on your inner workings. On your breath. Or on how you don't beat your heart, but rather *it beats you.*

You may discover the path to spiritual, and often physical, wellness—a real faith in Life.

Between your thoughts (and heartbeats), where you wouldn't think you'd find anything, you can actually find *everything*—like the objects of your deepest devotion; your soul's expression, your inner purpose; the meaning of spiritual evolution. . .and maybe even dig for the greatest treasure of all—Love. Then you'll probably find out that it was all around you in plain sight, all the time.

Say . . . I guess that would qualify meditation as another official tip for finding true happiness—and a very good one at that, as it is the wellspring of joy, serenity, self-awareness, wholeness, and Love available to everyone.

Here's an anecdote about the Buddha, who became *the* expert on finding inner peace and oneness after spending about seven solid years in meditation. When a skeptic asked the Buddha: "What have you gained through meditation?" the Buddha replied: "Nothing at all."

"Then, Blessed One, what good is it?" the skeptic asked.

"Let me tell you what I lost through meditation," the Buddha answered. "Sickness, anger, depression, insecurity, the burden of old age, the fear of death. *That* is the good of meditation."

One very important thing I learned in my first NDE was that *thought*—in the life after this one—*is not the same thing as it seems to be here.* There was no demanding, sequential voice in my mind that "kept me in line." No internal labels or judgments that I can recall. I didn't even seem to have a lot to think about; yet I definitely had thoughts. They were just much easier. Less intensely purposeful. My understanding seemed balanced and holistic. My thinking there was a lot more like my thinking here is during and after meditation. Calm and easy.

When you approach meditation and contemplation with willingness and a kind of pleasant curiosity, and allow yourself to explore the world within, a whole new universe of possibility starts to open up—one that you may have only suspected was there until now. That time alone turns out to be time very well spent. The more you meditate, the more you find a kind of calm but alive space in place of all those messy thoughts that simply don't work for you anymore. You get complete acceptance of situations and people that may have made you a bit crazy at one time. There's always that shimmering light inside your closed eyes, that inner theater where the Universe plays its endless movie about the wonder of Life.

You can dip your toe directly into the spiritual world that's just inside your closed eyes, in between your thoughts, which is the place where we seem to be coming from and going to after all. This is "the stuff that dreams are made of." The effervescent energy that Life is made of: Unified Consciousness, or Nirvana, or the Kingdom of Heaven, or whatever you want to call it. It's where we're all connected, in that ocean of Love I've been talking about all along.

And while you're dipping your toe, you may begin to notice something else—that you are not alone there either. That you never have been really alone, and that you never will be. You can find that all the souls you have loved, who have loved you and have meant something in your life, can all be with you there, looking over your shoulder. Ever-present in your life. Speaking softly into your inner ear with quiet encouragement.

Are those voices that you can hear in there—of your angels and ancestors and spirit guides, your father and mother, your heroes and *higher self*—all just figments of your imagination? Or are they all really standing right alongside you, in another dimension that we'll all be able to see soon enough?

Does it matter? You can still hear them and speak with them right now if you listen and speak in the right way—and it does make for very pleasant conversation. You can hear them in your mind when you're not thinking, and feel them in your heart when you're *open* in that way. And they will all love you anyway, whether you believe they're only in your imagination or not.

# The Third Tip
# for True Happiness

And about time for it too, especially when we don't have as much control over our lives as we'd like—including those times when we're in an unhappy location, or confronting a set of sad circumstances, or dealing with serious physical pain. Those times when finding happiness seems like a real impossibility. Radical kindness and radical forgiveness can go a long way to transform any unhappy conditions into happier ones. But right now seems the perfect time to introduce my third official tip for finding happiness in the particularly difficult times. It has the not-so-fun-sounding title of *radical surrender.*

It doesn't sound like much fun, because there's usually a negative connotation to the verb "surrender," although most of us have known times in our lives when that word may have suggested more bliss than anything else. So let's go with that—the blissful definition. Because when we are really catching some poop—when we are really going through dark, tough stuff; when everything is being stood on its head—perhaps that's a good time to stand some of our usual definitions on their heads as well.

With that in mind, I don't mean surrender in the sense of resignation, or of "giving up" or losing in a pejorative sense; I mean it rather in the sense of surrender as *a strategy,* as a way to deal with life on Life's terms. Surrender in the sense of joining up with the winning side. So, instead of confronting and struggling and fighting a relentlessly difficult losing battle, surrender it to the Universe (or to God, or to whatever you like) and allow yourself the means to change yourself over and discover happiness in the aftermath—which isn't really the end of anything, except perhaps suffering.

All through human experience, as part of the quest for wholeness and happiness, there's been the inevitable need to pass through "the darkest hour" to reach the place of light—the place of acceptance, of self-love, of Love and compassion for others. In short, the place of happiness. That darkness will happen in every life—at the beginning, in the middle, or at "the end"—so resisting it will only give it more power.

Here's that ironically funny, but suitable, suggestic[...] "When you're going through Hell, *keep going!*" Des[...] urge to flounder in the feeling that you're meeting son[...] rible *end*, allow yourself to realize that you may just be [...]ss-ing through some horrible *middle*. You'll be out of it soon enough. Even bad stuff doesn't last forever (though it tends to feel as if it does). "This too shall pass." Here's another one: "If you're paddling too hard upriver, turn around and go downstream." That's an accurate, and appropriately easy, metaphor for radical surrender—simply to allow Life to carry you along in its stream.

When you look back at the hardest times in your life, you see that they're over, aren't they? And you are still here; and you will still be here, whether *here* happens to be Cleveland, or some transcendent celestial dimension (what the heck, aim high). Surrendering to your broken-openness, releasing your sense of suffering, releases something else as well—something mysterious that allows growth and healing energy in through that very same break in your human shell, like a wildflower growing through a crack in the pavement. It allows that energy of the Universe that flows through all of Life to lift us up from beneath, wrap around us, flow through us, and carry us along with it. Like swimming in Love.

Understandably, you'll never want to go through a dif-ficult time quite like that again and, because of the wis-dom you've gained from surrendering, you may never have to. Certainly, not in the same way. You're burning up that karma, taking the action. And yes, surrender is an abso-lutely necessary action to take, in order to leave the pain behind and to grow into an easier, more graceful way to live. But like radical kindness and radical forgiveness, radical surrender is an effort you have to make in order to benefit from it. It also takes a little work for a very big pay-off.

And of course, you really shouldn't go through it alone. We know we don't have to go through anything alone. And if you feel as if you should go through it alone, as if you don't want to impose your difficulties on anyone else, then you're just being selfish again and what you really need is *more* surrender, in the sense of gratefully accepting the company and care of others. That can be a big leap for some of the more self-reliant of us—just accepting help. But what a pleasure it is to relax and let someone care for you. There's a big well-deserved pay-off in receiving as well. It's how the circle of giving and receiving comes back around and creates wholeness. It's simple and yet it's elegant, right? And we always like elegant . . .

A painful illness or injury, or a long convalescence, may deprive us of many aspects of life that we can no longer enjoy the way we once did—playing tennis, or carrying furniture up and down three flights of stairs. But if we create a new strategy for happiness by "doubling-down" (forgive a little gambling parlance) on our effort to find serenity, fellowship, compassion, humor, generosity, and all the rest of those ever-reliable spiritual tools that require no physicality at all, that ocean of Love will carry us, weightlessly. Once again, if we look for *what we can do for somebody else*— always as counterintuitive as it may sound—we may suddenly find that we can almost entirely escape the constraints and discomforts of gravity itself, and begin to inhabit the dimension of Love "that flesh is heir to," as Shakespeare would say. It may sound kind of unscientific, but it's true.

It can get a little dark—just until the sun comes back up, that is—and so we find faith in our knowledge of the way the Universe is always working to return us back to the source of Love.

While we usually equate the need to surrender with some fight that we're losing, surrender especially works when we're not even in a fight—that is, when things are going well. At those times, we're in a natural state of surrender because, of course, there's no reason to be struggling. When things are going well, everything seems to go smoothly and life seems easy. So notice how, when things aren't at all bad, surrender is *already* connected to happiness, and to the attitudes that allow flowing happiness (and Love) to carry us along.

The same thing is true of my other two official tips—kindness and forgiveness are always already included in real happiness. So it's not that we're building more stuff into our lives in order to reach happiness; we're simplifying things back to their Source. In short, happiness is always waiting for us to simply get out of our own way, and find out that we've had it all along.

# The Hardest Part Is Always the Parting Part

We all know that there is no easy way to say goodbye to the ones we love, to those life partners we've loved to be with—even if it's only for a little while, much less "forever." I harbor a deep belief that we've always known one another. And although I'm quite certain that we'll meet again, I can't guarantee to you that you'll be reunited with everyone you've ever loved after you transition over to "the other side"—at least, not based on my somewhat limited personal experience. My second NDE only featured brief scenes from my life, but there have been plenty of other folks who've "come back" and reported that they spent quality time with their loved ones in the life after this one. Knowing that life continues after this, I'm certain they've been telling us what we can reliably expect to look forward to.

It sure seems to me that we've known one another before, and probably will again, and that we're here to help each other learn our lessons through who knows how many lives, all pre-arranged in some way (however the heck time works).

Losing one we love is life's most deeply difficult experience. In an instant, a life that means everything to us is suddenly defined in the past tense. We (and this world) are irreversibly deprived of that unique presence. That beloved spirit has escaped these confines, and in that emotional wake we are left to face our real limitations. Involuntarily, we bear witness to a period of intense extra-dimensional gravity that feels a lot as if all the oxygen has been sucked out of the world—because, in a way, it has. That core sustenance, that essential support, that eternal reason for being is suddenly gone; and yet we must continue, even though we may not feel like it at all. We must continue, *because all life does*. That eternal reason for being still exists; it's just that getting past the loss feels like an impossibility for a while.

In the chapter about pain, I gave a formula for the cure to heartbreak, and that's what loss is about—brokenheartedness. We've been deprived of that which we love with an unconditionality that trumps all other experience; and being without it or replacing it seems out of the question. But really, the same formula applies—the basics of repairing our hearts and finding new reasons for living. It takes *time,* and the evidence of survival that time gives us— the continued presence of sensation, of identification, of joy. Moving through the trauma that's acknowledged in the experience of *grieving,* and allowing those sensations their rightful time and place.

It requires *gratitude* (as counterintuitive as it sounds) for the experience of that life that we've lost—for the grounding completeness and connection to the medium of Love that it has given us. That enrichment, that connection, is now something that can never be taken away from us. We've earned that understanding of Life's potential by having experienced Love like that, and having survived through to the meaning it's irrevocably brought into our lives. In a new way, it makes it possible for us to witness the beauty of nature, the wonder of one another, and the unlimited potential that the medium of Love always provides us, without fail. The powerful humility that we're granted through our loss makes a far richer perception of Life available to us.

With time and gratitude, we begin to realize the opportunity our loss opens up for us—the chance to carry on that deep purpose for living, the completeness that comes from witnessing the material cycle of Love's presence in this life. We learn what it takes to carry on, and can support others through their losses with that knowledge. The spirits of our loved ones "passed" *want us* to recover from our suffering in this way—by passing along the power of Love we share, beyond the shallow constraints of life and "death." They don't want us to suffer needlessly.

Then, you'll come to know in your heart that that person (or that wonderful pet) that you love, though physically gone, is still alive in a spiritual dimension greater than this one. They've just matriculated, extra-dimensionally, so to speak.

Although they're missing and very missed in your material life, there's that reality of their never really having left you, of their being alive in a place that's always accessible through your heart. The more you consciously and intentionally choose that living heart connection to them— the more you engage your spirit in the trans-dimensional medium of Love— the more vividly present they will be in your heart and in your life. They *are* alive, beyond this world; so *let them be alive*. In fact, you can even keep right on talking to them as if they'd never left.

I do suggest that you do this privately, in order to prevent arrest and possible institutionalization—although, with all the people you see walking down the street carrying on electronic conversations with the open air, I think you can probably get away with it. Anyway, I'm sure your loved ones will understand.

Of course, it'll never be quite the same thing as having them there physically with you, so it's necessary to carry them in your heart with very great intention. It takes real effort to overcome that barrier to one another's love that death seems to create; but the greater your intention, the greater your understanding and belief of their living pres-

How to Survive Life (and Death)

ence in your heart, the more you will experience them everyday. If you make them an object of your inner devotion, then the quieter you are inwardly, the more you will open your heart and allow their presence—and the more clearly you will hear them and know that they are forever available to you.

Our human life is a physical, sensory experience, so it's only natural to experience physical memories of those we've lost—their energy and their touch. Time is the only thing that will diminish those sensations; but in the meantime, we have to concentrate on what that Love felt like, not on what we've lost. Like all spiritual practices, the clarity of contact waxes and wanes through this veil of what the Hindu call *maya*—the clunky obstructions of this life form. Like all spiritual practices, it once again depends on practice, practice, practice. If you're willing to work past that insistent, slightly selfish (even romantic) state of loss, *you will find that they are present,* and that, when you need them, they are there to help you.

My educated guess is that it works that way from the other side as well. As in this life, one of the most important things you will ever need to do in the next is to really listen, and *be present*. So pay attention once you're "dead." Look alive! We will always be able to help those we love through Love, wherever we are.

Parting with loved ones is definitely the hardest part about the whole process, whether they leave you or vice versa. In a way, it's harder to be left behind, with that predictable, unnecessary human urge to blame ourselves for everything. It really just means that we must carry on in this sometimes difficult life without that blessed physical partnership. (I don't mean to speak for anyone else, but I know that I can be pretty useful that way myself sometimes—especially when it comes to paying bills, cooking Mexican food, and carrying heavy stuff.) If it's you that's moving on, let your loved ones know that they're not to blame for anything. Let them know that you are not abandoning them and that you will be beaming Love right into their hearts in an extra-dimensional fashion. Look them in the eyes and tell them something like:

> I love you, and I will always be loving you, so keep me in your heart, and you will be in mine. But *live!* Go past the sadness, and try not to suffer. Enjoy each moment the best way you can! And know that I'll be there, always nearby—unless I'm busy somewhere else, in which case just make sure that it's important if you call, and give me as much advance notice as you can.

We do all get busy, you know, on "the other side"—just like all of those quiet, helpful angels.

At some point in our lives, we all may have to inhabit that peculiar bubble of time where we're called upon to witness the passage of a life. It's possibly the most difficult, but most essential, thing we have to do—showing up for an event we dread and knowing how to conduct ourselves through this unmistakably *sacred* time. A lot of odd feelings may get kicked up when we're called upon to be caregivers, or to be taken care *of*. Feelings like powerlessness and blame, or even resentment and anger at the "unfairness" of it all. But really, it is the fairest part of Life, that moment when we must come to terms with mortality. Intuitively, we know that we must *be there for that*—that we must surrender into our circumstances, experience our grief, and rise above our self-centered feelings. Our feelings are, after all, just feelings. They are directing us to our truths, but they aren't necessarily the truth themselves.

It's just hard to find your footing, to find your proper place at that time, suspended in that sort of *grace*. But here's what you can always do to face the pain, to put your conflicting feelings in their proper place and make your role and purpose clear and comfortable: Push everything else aside, and join your heart to *Love*. Within the fundamental understanding that there is no death, Love will always provide you intuitively with sure sanity, support, purpose, and direction.

Compassionate identification with one another is our connection to that healing power as part of the circuit—the circular, mutual, spiritual agreement between the person who needs the healing most and the person who has the chance to bring it to them. The truth is that *everyone* needs the healing, and so it's that identification we experience with one another that is the real key to supplying the aid and comfort—the "spiritual medicine"—that can only be passed from one being to another. *We* are the vehicles of this powerful spiritual energy. Like waterwheels, as we collect the energy of Love and compassion in our lives, Life brings us around into position to pour it out for another.

You may just call it the Golden Rule, because that's what it is. (When something's given a name like "the Golden Rule," it's usually earned the name.) We're always being given the chance to become the person who does unto another the very things that we'd be most grateful to receive ourselves. And given the circular nature of Life, we'll get our chance for that as well. Meanwhile, what might be considered one of Life's most painful episodes is really the opportunity to provide one of its greatest rewards—the fulfillment of that most sacred agreement that we've made with each other, somewhere, someplace in time.

When we willingly (or even sometimes not so willingly) take part in this eternal cycle of caring, I think we become intuitively aware of the invisible spiritual machinery at work in the world and in our lives here on this planet. As so many revered spiritual texts have told us, *giving*—being of service to another, setting aside all selfish concerns we may naturally have—gives us more of Life's precious intangible rewards than anything else possibly can. Healing and comfort, and—here it is again—Love. And it works both ways—to care and to be cared for.

The Universe (God, if you will) suspends us in this bubble of grace at those times, especially at the end of one or another's life, when all materiality fades into insignificance and the pure spirit owns us completely and irrevocably. We are connected to the divine magic of Love and Life when we bear witness to that transition of the spirit out of the painful body, and back into that joyful light of being and bliss.

Now, remember your experiences when your friends were sick and appeared to be "on their last legs"? Think of how the others around you must be feeling if it's you who are there now. That's always been an undeniably difficult situation for anyone to handle. And what is it that always makes difficult situations go more easily? Why, *laughter*, of course. We all know that there is categorically no time when humor isn't a very welcome addition . . . a godsend, in fact.

Certainly dying isn't generally thought of as being very funny. In fact, no one (except maybe a stand-up comedian) is really allowed to be funny about it, with the exception of the one who's actually doing it. Then it can be as funny as you want to make it. And if you're prone to pulling a leg now and then, you've got a big advantage at a time like that—the element of surprise. If it is you who are dying, believe me, no one is expecting you to be funny, so maybe you can do the unexpected. Don't take yourself so seriously that you can't lighten things up a little. And if it's meant for someone else's benefit, the same is true again: light-heartedness allows more light to enter into any dark situation.

Have you ever found yourself just totally "losing it" right at a very serious moment, and busting out in hilarious laughter? It feels great, even though it can be so wrong.

Lots of times, it's those "serious" moments that need busting open the most! It may always be so right . . . when it's so wrong.

Lots of people send you flowers when you're sick. Why not do the unexpected? Send *them* flowers first, with a card that says: "Thank you for being the best friend a person could ever have!" Or, "You have improved my life so much—whether I wanted you to or not." Or, "It makes me saddest to think that I will still have more hair than you." Say *au revoir* with a little style. A little originality. It's not the time to forget your manners, but it's also not the time to forget what has made you love each other all along. Besides, think of what inspiration others will get from your positive spirit, and what a nice fare-thee-well it'll be—and of all the nice things they'll say afterward if it's you who's shuffling off this mortal coil.

If you've still got some clumsy situation left dangling— not really a grudge, so to speak, but maybe a friend borrowing something kind of big (like a kayak, for example) and not returning it—drop your friend a note letting him or her off the hook. Something like this (whether it's true or not):

> Dear Jim,
> I lent you my kayak, which is fine. Don't worry about it. In fact, I only ever used it a couple of times—so I'd like you to keep it, and put it to good use. It always seemed a little too heavy to me. Blessings to you, my friend! See you down river!

*Now* is always a good time to be generous with everything—your stuff, your humor, your spirit, your Love. And especially the *things* you don't need anymore. Give to your family. Give to friends, or to strangers. Give to someone who really needs it. Give to someone who maybe doesn't need it at all. I mean, who needs it? Just give, as a token of your sincere esteem, and as a nod to the ever-reincarnating spirit of recycling.

Being especially magnanimous has always been a nice way to say hello, or goodbye. Or *au revoir*. Or *auf wiedersehen*. Or *hasta la vista*. You'll notice that, in many languages, saying goodbye is never really saying goodbye at all—it's more like "until the next time," or "when we meet again." It's as if we all knew it already. My all-time favorite is *Aloha*. In Hawaiian, *Alo* means "presence," and *Ha* means "breath." So *Aloha* means "presence of breath." Of course, it works very well in our context (in and out), because everyone knows that *Aloha* means both—hello and goodbye.

By now, I must have mentioned being "open-hearted" at least half a dozen times, so let me talk about what I really mean when I say that—and why it's especially important when it comes to this most difficult part of losing, or leaving, one another (for the time being).

We've all experienced moments of spontaneous open-heartedness—when one of our kids makes us extremely proud; while experiencing a particularly transcendent piece of music; when seeing a great big dog allow a tiny kitten to fall asleep on its head. That's the feeling I'm talking about. It's the sensation you get when your thoughts instantly turn off and your heart wells up instinctively with Love and compassion. We suddenly occupy a place within ourselves where we automatically allow Life to be simply what it is. An incredibly easy place of complete tolerance, acceptance, willingness, and compassion. There's *joy* there—and no place for resentment, or envy, or fear. Without even thinking, we find ourselves empowered by Love. The trick then is to sustain that feeling, and to try to make it our primary state of being. Meditation on the sources of our devotion helps us open this beautiful passageway to wholeness, and to keep it open.

This open-heartedness is particularly important for us to help counteract the irreversible loss we incur when death comes along, because it's the only comfortable and effective way we have to surrender to the true theme of this book: There is *no such thing* as death—aside from having our bodies poop out. Open-heartedness is the only certain path to finding the necessary faith to look past the pain of loss (beyond our bodies giving it up) to the knowledge that we will never end our being for each other eternally—where "eternity" isn't some timeline going on and on, but instead a state of forever being and living right in this moment.

While I'm not usually big on exercises, here's an exercise for opening your heart that you can revisit to help keep it open:

> Stand up and, in an imaginary way (please), grab the seam right over your solar plexus with both hands and open up your chest as if you were opening a great coat.
>
> Now *breathe out* and let all the energy of your heart pour out!
>
> Then *breathe in* and let everything external that's full of beauty and light and sadness *enter*.
>
> Now keep breathing, and try to stay breathing for as long as you can.

That's the only physical exercise in the book, so you can sit back down.

When we make open-heartedness our way of life, our lives expand and overlap in that fourth-dimensional way, no matter how much time we have left together. We can co-own our Love, our sadness, and our hopes with everyone and everything at once. We realize a new kind of mixing-together, a new identification with life. Even formerly small and emotionally confined lives become huge and joyful and celebratory. They can grow to contain all those we've loved, all those we may love, and all the Life that we share with every person and every creature we know—or even those we don't know. Because, when we're completely open-hearted, we can know and understand everyone and everything.

Entering into the most difficult passages of Life becomes a whole new basket of eggs when we enter into them willingly and open-heartedly. Because, when we expand our heart energy, our compassionate consciousness expands as well, and we can easily connect solidly to that precious, focused power of Love—the kind we naturally want to share when we only have a little time remaining together.

Life, writ even larger, is clearly much too big a thing for this one little bubble-life of ours to contain. We can only be contained *by it,* now and forever-more. Once we know that, we begin to occupy the "fourth dimension," where we will continue to live with our loved ones—to love them, to be guided by them, to live in their hearts, and to have them live in ours.

# How Dark Does "The Darkest" Have to Get?

"Yeshua said: Blessed are those who have undergone ordeals. They have entered into life."

Logion 5823, *Gospel of Thomas*

Here comes the hardest part. You can skip it, unless you feel as if you really need to be here. It's about the physical reality of dying.

I'm sad to say that there were years of my life that I spent in a gradually enveloping darkness of the spirit— years when I had to live through an intense, inescapable psychic pain in order to find my way out, to emerge back into the light. I can't recommend it. In retrospect, it bordered on a death of the soul, when I may perhaps have been closer to actually dying more often than I cared to allow during those difficult years. I feel regret in saying that—and I do regret that lost time—but I certainly don't regret having gotten through it.

At times, like many people, I've had to endure terrible physical pain that seemed never-ending, but that, in truth, lasted only a few months at most. I was fairly young throughout those struggles, and the three physical "brushes with death" I describe in these pages were sudden and unexpected, and only lasted a relatively short time. None of them compares to a prolonged and painful decline. My experience of profound hopelessness has been limited to those periods of personal despair I've known in my life— periods through which I was always pretty sure I'd see the morning sun again, eventually.

Many of us are likely to experience these times in our lives—times of seemingly relentless pain, despair, and isolation within what seem to be the prisons of our beings. This is what many of us truly fear regarding the end of our lives—not death so much as the possibility of a painful, helpless decline, when living seems worse than anything death may have to offer (which, I believe, is the truth) and, as it happens, when there *will* be no end to it until it is over. This is too often the case before we leave this life; but it will not last forever.

In truth, I don't think that any of us will ever comprehend the courage and strength of spirit required to endure the prolonged assault on a person's comfort, well-being, and dignity—on a person's very humanity, as dying from this life can sometimes bring on—until we face it ourselves. There can be no more solemn measure of a person, nor need for the presence of Love, more than at that time when practically everything that Life has given is taken back. Forgive me if I am describing circumstances that are immediately familiar to you. I have never meant to skip blithely over the real pain that Life, for some hard-to-know reason, seems to require so many of us to endure on our way *through*.

I've been describing the weaving of the back half of this life together with the front part of a promised "Life to come" as if it were a dolphin, swimming through the ocean of this life and leaping into the heavens of the next, without ever really acknowledging the darker parts of this life where we find ourselves dispassionately pinned to the bottom and truly suffering. I'm sorry if I haven't acknowledged this yet with the serious compassion that it deserves.

I don't believe that there's any easy way past the real sense of abandonment we may have—or the feelings of betrayal, or humiliation, or victimization, or *loss*—except an even greater dependence on some form of Love as the only answer—on the willingness to humbly ask for help, to rely humbly on the *Divine*. There is pain that even Love cannot abate; but there is so much that it can bear, and there is, in fact, a kind of sacred access to Love—even a very special, divine *generation* of Love—that takes place in our moments of truth.

The hardest thing of all is suffering the pain that exists in what feels like loveless darkness, even if we know that darkness is only temporarily concealing a beautiful picture we just can't see yet. Still, having faith in that Love seems a lot to ask. Yet *faith is not always a well-lit place.* In fact, more often than not, it's not. Each of us will experience powerlessness and loss completely, will have to own them, and will learn the truths that only that clear light of humility can show us.

If you still naturally fear having to go there, welcome to the club. Here is all I can say to you: In the times when it seems impossible to carry on, know that *this too shall pass.* And know that what appears to be "the end" really *isn't.*

Then just look to the simplest wonders for the evidence—the sun on your hand, a bird singing, a slender tree swaying in the breeze—and recognize the beauty there within and underneath it all, in every moment. The beauty always blossoming within you, and within each of us. Life always opens up again, after it closes down. Like the dusk and dawn, and the moon waxing and waning, there will always be these simple miracles. Like life and death.

It's only right and proper, isn't it, that life uses us up and spends us, just as we so often feel we're doing ourselves to Life? In fact, I've heard it said that we don't live Life, rather Life *lives us.* (I think it was Joseph Campbell who said that, but Life has already lived me enough to have affected my memory.) It makes absolute sense, though, doesn't it? That we are reduced back to practically our simplest form, our physical energy depleted, all outward and external presentations wrapped up not so neatly? We are returned to more or less the elements that we were constructed from in the first place, just a little worse for the wear. I guess we have to expect that it might not be such a pretty or painless process, though there've always been more than a few pretty fabulous things about it all.

To me, with my experience of the blissful nature of the afterlife, to make it a crime for individuals to personally choose a controlled end to their lives, or for them to give that power to a trusted loved one, is totally idiotic. To prevent an adult who's already managed to live his or her entire life from deservedly escaping the pain of a prolonged, helpless decline into the joyful comfort of the world beyond this one—*that* should be the crime. As long as love and reason are involved, the decision of dispensing with a useless and painful vehicle should irrevocably rest with its occupant. At that point, the body is finished. If it's a spirit's choice to leave it, and the mind and heart are settled, then so be it.

Life only wishes to reclaim "the clear bead at the center" (as Rumi calls it), the inner *you* that exists after this, in our new form of wholeness and grace. What you want to do with your old body is your business, and your business alone.

A true story to finish here, about a very famous and success-ful man, and his sweet and sadly painful experience with (Life and) death.

He began life humbly, but became enormously successful in his field. He fell in love and married a beautiful woman, and she gave birth to beautiful twin boys. His career took him to very high places indeed—to world fame, in fact—but as it did, his wife began to struggle with a subtle but pro-gressive mental illness. Then, tragically, one their twin sons died suddenly at just twenty years old. His wife went into a steep decline and began to waste away. Two years later, she died.

The man picked himself up, moved on, and continued life with great success, piling up ever more prestigious accomplishments one on top of the other. When he reached the point where many men are at the top of their games, he was diagnosed with pancreatic cancer and given very little time to live. His physical state began to decline, but those closest to him claim that he had a spirit and an energetic presence in his Life that allowed him to live much longer than the doctors had given him.

In his last days, he continually joked with his family and with visiting friends, putting them all at ease. And when, after painful months, he finally passed on over, according to his son his last smiling words were: "Bliss . . . bliss."

This man's entire life (and his graceful passing) are an inspiration to millions, and I firmly believe that his indefatigable human spirit lives on in this ocean of Love that is Life, reunited with his beloved and with the common Source of us all.

# The Last Time I Checked (Out), I Was in Arizona

If one's passing isn't the result of normal wear and tear in the course of a long and eventful life, then it's most likely the result of a number of different unforeseeable factors converging in an unfortunate combination of poor health, bad luck, and wrong choices. My third, and hopefully final, Near Death Experience was two out of these three. I was in pretty good health—up until then, that is—but the combined elements of my life to that point led to my roughest transition.

I had returned to Arizona to lay desperate claim to a kind of false love that I'd kept waiting for a couple of years. A woman with a difficult past had been holding the door open for me, and now was threatening to slam it shut. I came to a fearful, unsure realization that a life with love was better than one without it, and I delusionally jumped at the opportunity to "fix myself" again (despite the red flags). It had been a number of years after the last NDE I described and, although I'd learned a lot of important lessons in Life, apparently none of them had sunk in quite deep enough yet. After years of denying all the evidence of my spiritual life, I was living in what amounted to an unconsciously selfish, fearful, loveless world.

Arizona is renowned for a kind of Western lawlessness and anarchy, and I was about to come face to face with it on this particular Super Bowl Sunday. I'd gone to watch the game with some friends on Main Street in a medium-size college town and, immediately afterward, went to use a pay phone in a crowded plaza that was alive with post-game festivities. (There were pay phones, back then.) My fianceé was back at her apartment baking scones.

The moment I called her up on the pay phone, I became the target of a very large, somewhat inebriated "skinhead's" attentions. If you aren't familiar with skinheads, they are a particularly violent group of disaffected young men who often have links to pseudo-military and neo-nazi interests. There's a lot of that in Arizona, God bless 'em. Having just returned from back East, I was dressed fairly nicely by local standards, which I guess is what attracted this fellow's scrutiny and ire.

Before I knew what was hitting me, this great big kid was *hitting* me, hollering sexual epithets in my face, and pushing me back until the phone cable was stretched tight. Then he reached over and hung up the phone, shouting in my face. I managed to calm him down a little, assuring him that I had been on the phone with my fianceé, and so I wasn't whatever he thought I was that had so enraged him—which I guess was gay. Finally, he cooled off, turned, and wandered away.

I got back on the phone with my fianceé, who had heard the whole thing transpire, and, believing my attacker to be out of earshot, I began to describe the whole crazy episode to her. Apparently, the skinhead wasn't completely out of earshot. The next thing I knew, I was being attacked again, only much more aggressively than the first time. I dropped the phone as he shoved me hard, bearing down on me furiously, his veins popping out and his fists clenched.

Then, on top of being in the wrong place at the wrong time, I made one of the worst choices of my life. Without really thinking (reacting out of fear), I instinctively planted my back foot and landed a driving punch hard on the kid's chin. He straightened up stiffly and rocked back onto his heels, hands down to his sides, fingers outstretched. Deserving a cautionary cry of "timberrrr," the poor kid fell straight over backward, out cold. It was a lucky punch. That was the only lucky part of the evening for me.

Some onlookers lauded my "courage," but I was already making a run for it back to the bicycle I had ridden to town, in an effort to escape home to safety. I had no idea that the whole incident was being watched by an entire van full of skinheads, who, as I rode away, intercepted me and knocked me off my bike from behind, hitting me in the head very hard with some blunt object and sending me head first into the curb. Head first into a very dark pool full of hungry, smiling crocodiles.

A year and a half later, when the police report finally became available to me, I discovered that the local police had witnessed the skinheads' pursuit and assault of me, and then watched as they went back and forth to their van, returning to kick my unconscious body, as is their signature practice. Apparently, they even wear boots designed for such stompin'.

So much for the local police, who, as it turned out, shared the same regional military background as some of my assailants—as well as the same kind of boots.

Once again, I wasn't in this world. But unlike before, I wasn't free of it either. There was no easy sense of liberation or comfortably numb detachment, as there had been in my previous experiences. I wasn't consciously present for the stomping or for the eventual emergency medical procedures on my behalf, but I was strangely aware of the grim, grinding physicality of it all. This was not an easy transition; in fact, I knew it was not going to be a transition at all, even though I definitely *wanted* it to be. Something was not nearly as welcoming as it had been before.

If you can wear out your welcome "on the other side," I guess that's what had happened, because I wasn't in a place of lightness at all. It was more like a dark holding room.

There was a gentle but firm presence, but it wasn't telling me anything I wanted to hear. I did not want to go back this time and I remember struggling against it—the struggle becoming conflated with the sensations of waking physical trauma. But this time, I had to go back. I had no choice in the matter. Nothing had been appropriate about the means of my departure, and I had a lot to do before I could find any relief in "death." That was the sense of the whole thing—that in the intervening years since my previous experiences, I had not been doing very much right.

When I finally lost the struggle to stay where I was, it seemed as if I almost immediately came to lying on the sidewalk, looking up into the searching eyes of an emergency medical technician. "He's *back*," he said, as in "He's returned to this life."

A friend who's been an EMS worker for years later assured me that this going and coming back is something he's witnessed many, many times.

Along with other injuries, I was badly concussed (again) and had another big scar in almost the same place on the left side of my head—which brings up interesting questions about injuries to either hemisphere of the brain. Do injuries to the left side of the brain—the ordering, calculating, and comparing side—enhance a dominance of the right side of the brain—the non-analytical, non-judgemental, "in-the-moment," "spiritual," and creative side? Modern neuroanatomy may suggest so. I'm no real expert on those questions, but it is interesting, isn't it?

It took months—no, actually, it took *years*—for me to recover. I needed surgery (again) to repair my massacred shoulder, titanium pins to hold me together, and all that. But I did get one new ability out of it: My trick shoulder can pretty reliably predict the approach of heavy weather, so there *is* always a silver lining.

I also learned a few really important lessons in the whole painful affair. In dealing with the authorities at the time, I'd had to come to terms with the fact that there was nothing I could do about it. That there wasn't going to be any justice for me, whether I was "right" or not. The witnesses were all gone. Officially, the city only had a case against *me,* for actually striking the first blow. The police made it clear that they were not going to be helpful to my cause, so I would have made a lot of enemies in the wrong places if I had pursued the matter any further.

In short, sometimes there is no right or wrong; there just *is.* The world happens in the way it happens, and it isn't about me—except in the way I choose to energize the circumstances of my life. It was a bad time that came about as a result of an odd collision of factors, catalyzed by my reaction to them; and in order to move on, I simply needed to forgive the Universe (it didn't mind) and be grateful for the lessons learned. That took a little while. In fact, it took *years.*

Here's one lesson I definitely learned the hard way: *Violence (of any sort) never solves anything.* It is only mirrored by more violence. Energizing any situation with psychological or physical violence leads only to immediate suffering, and more remorseful suffering after the fact. Only Love can ever really work to defuse a confrontation; in fact, every serious problem has a spiritual solution.

What were the deeper lessons I learned in this episode? First, there are a few things each of us needs to accomplish here in this life—preferably *good* things—and, as you might suspect, the more the better. We're here to complete ourselves by finding Love, and to help complete others by giving it. That means we are part of a great nurturing and supportive (though not always "fair") cycle of being in which we are all playing our roles—an intelligence of immense wisdom and compassion that keeps track of our progress and gives us our purpose in this life. The closer we live to being our true selves, but the less we put ourselves at the center, the easier it will be to know how we may best serve that purpose.

Perhaps the scariest, but most awe-inspiring (and comforting), realization I finally reached—long after all my bumps and bruises had subsided—has also been the hardest one for me to wrap my head around and to actually learn to live with. It's the part I mentioned earlier that has to do with *really* never getting any privacy (in a way that has probably crossed everyone's mind at one time or another).

Years later, when I came to the point where I could turn the corner on all the pain I'd suffered and caused in my life, I was hit by something I'd known all along—something very, very moving: *Someone had been with me each time I nearly died.* Someone had gently shepherded me away from my wrecked car; someone had shown me those scrupulously selected scenes of great significance from my life; and someone had gently, but forcefully, pushed me back into this life to tell you what I'm telling you now. I've realized now that it was *one* someone—my guide, my guardian, my angel—whom I have finally come to know personally (like a lost and loving aunt). I'm certain that we all have one, and that we are all receiving that same kind of personal attention. We are *never alone.*

Now, we all know why that's scary. I mean, really, somebody's watching me *all* the time? That's right. But it's no big deal because, fortunately, I'm not particularly important, and neither are you. Nobody is, yet everybody is.

And "all the time" is nothing really. I believe that our angels observe us from a perspective *apart* from time. I believe they can see every one of those life moments eternally, as they happen, like discreet panes of time suspended in space—in much the same way that those moments can suspend themselves in our memories. All of this is happening *now.* All of it has always been happening now, and always will. Being human makes this impossible to see. Yet, in our hearts, each of us knows the cause and effect of all these moments strung together, especially when we concede to this intimate exposure of the truth. We know the parts of our lives that need mending, the edges that need smoothing, the loose ends that need to be bound.

Who really wants a witness to all their *stuff,* regardless of how forgiving that witness may be? It's been said that "your sickness lies in your secrets"—your misdeeds, selfishness, hostile thoughts, and all that stuff we "safely" hide in our little compartments. Being human makes us want to believe that no one can see it written on our faces, or veiled in our desires, or behind our actions. But, of course, they do. That's *who we are,* on the outside. The question is, who are we really; and who are we going to be? Those self-revealing secrets shouldn't cause us fear, because we're actually keeping them *so we can learn from them.* Life doesn't happen *to you . . .*

Our angels (and angelic people) immediately forgive our misdeeds because they, too, know them so well. In this way, our fears can be dissolved into the reality of that profound intimacy—that shared knowledge of our greater selves. The Sufis call it *fana,* the dissolving of the human self into Eternal Love. That's nice, isn't it?

I think it was a great Swami named Maharshi who said that we don't fear death because of the painful end of life. By that time, many of us are ready for it. What we're never ready for is that painful accounting for what we've been up to, that golden interview. It's an embarrassment we naturally wish to avoid, again. So death *is* a blissful relief, but it can be made even more blissful by the way we live.

All of this helps me describe the hidden, but always available, *technology of the heart* that I've been talking about. It's all part of that greater reality that we're actually occupying—the realm of the spirit that constantly enfolds, supports, and directs us—and to which we and all of Life belong. But you already knew that.

Still, I hope they haven't been watching *everything* . . .

Not to scare you any more than the idea of being watched all the time, but in the context of my last moments in Arizona, it is clear to me that there are real consequences to being bad—both now and later. It just simply is not good. Being self-centered, cruel, violent, *unconscious* will deliver us to a "darker" place, in this life or the next, than where we might be able to live otherwise. How much darker is up to you, what you've done in Life, and how hard you're willing to look at yourself.

It comes as no surprise, does it? There simply are better ways to live and better ways to die, and one has everything to do with the other. And as I've found out about ways to die, exiting on a bad note is not the best way to get there.

The way this physicality is imbued with life energy—the means of our animation and of our sensual awareness—is all achieved by a pretty particular set of forces. And it won't do to go about releasing it all willy-nilly, or without some consideration and some proper well-deserved reason. It may require effort.

Personally, along with the very clear lessons I've learned through my own experiences, I find a lot of resonance in the wisdom of the ancient masters when it comes to the possibilities for our future, our past, and our present. And how can you go wrong with the good old ancient masters, for crying out loud? So, as best I can (and preposterous as it may seem), I'm going to try to describe what the three "fatal" experiences I've had have taught me about what may actually be the best way to go about "dying"—which (at the risk of sounding like a broken record) I don't believe is really dying, but actually just changing forms from this matter into a form of energy that grows out beyond our current constraints into an entirely different dimension of being.

I hope that, by now, you see that this is the central message of this whole book—what my experiences taught me and what I want to pass on to you: Simply that there's nothing to fear about dying. It's really a logical and beautiful culmination of Life, and quite a fluid process. And once you get past the rough patches you may have to cross to get there, you'll see, as well, that there is *no Death*.

# Exit at the Top— Or May We Have Our Check Now?

For centuries, high in the Himalayas, generations of holy men have dedicated their lives to understanding the worlds of the eternal self in some of the ways I touched on earlier. In India, *swamis* analyzed the forces that flow through us and connect us to the energies of the Earth, the Universe, and time. It may strike you that I'm getting mystical here, talking about swamis and all, and I am. These holy men (and women) have been on a singularly serious path. They don't watch TV, or go to the movies. They just selflessly dedicate their (many) lives to discovering the hidden secrets of our souls, so that we can learn from them.

What they discovered is a little esoteric and a bit complex by our standards. So, although I won't pretend to know everything about it all, I will make an effort to tailor the little bit I do know to fit into our common understanding, because there may be some unfamiliar cross-cultural ideas here for some.

Try not to head for the exits right away if you think this is all a little preposterous, because what I'm going to try to do now is to describe nothing less than the actual ways that our spirits may want to leave our bodies. I'm hoping that you'll cut me a little esoteric slack. (I've had some esoteric slacks in my time, but what I'm really asking is for you to bear with me.) Besides, I'm hoping that it will become clear to you intuitively just how well these ideas may actually work.

Have you ever heard of chakras? *Chakra* is an ancient Sanskrit word that means "wheel." It refers to one of the seven centers of internal energy located from the bottom to the top of the body's vertical axis. They're part of our internal spiritual energy system as defined by ancient Eastern practices, and are related to the energy "meridians" used in acupuncture and to the "chi" in T'ai Chi Chuan—that exercise you see many Chinese people doing in the town square early in the morning. The chakras provide us with a great way to relate our lives' motivations to these internal energy centers, showing us the types of issues that arise from each and then how we may be better able to classify, understand, and go about working with our issues and their driving forces.

This is where it'll get a little "alternatively" technical, and even a bit mystical, but please bear with me. There's some real wisdom in this approach. A quick look at the significance of each chakra, and I think you'll see the logic in it all. Besides, why would a nice monk or a friendly swami ever want to steer you wrong?

The first, lowest chakra is called the root chakra. It's situated at the base of your spine, where your tail would be if you had one (and I'm sure I probably did at some point). It relates to your fundamental sense of survival and will to exist, and so it's most important when you are getting a foothold early on in life. It's very basic.

The second chakra is located at your reproductive organs and has to do with the importance and quality of your sexual nature—the way in which the sex drive goes from being naturally instinctual, to influencing your personality and character. Becoming stuck in this chakra means never really growing past your sensory sexual attachments. It's a little like never getting out of high school. Ouch!

The third chakra is located at your navel, and has to do with taking life in (consuming and using it, as in *digesting it*) and keeping the operation and maintenance of life's functions in place. On the easy side, it's accomplishment and management; on the tough side, it's the willful need to control everything.

These are the three "lower" chakras, the ones that have to do with life's basic mechanisms. They're the practical, not-so-spiritual parts. As they become less necessary, when your essential energies wind down, on up the spirit ladder you go.

The fourth, or central or heart, chakra is the seat of involuntary, rhythmic functions like breathing and the beating of your heart that make your life completely possible. *Aloha,* "the presence of breath." It's also the origin and focus of your spiritual connection and evolution, because spiritually, it's where your *intuitive intelligence* and feelings arise—where you become open energetically to Life at a level above and beyond the lower instinctive, simply material levels.

The heart chakra is that inner chamber inhabited by our soul spirits—the gyroscopic nucleus through which we're connected to Love and the Universe. So if we're talking about being spiritually disconnected, this is where all our open-heartedness becomes possible. And our spiritual growth is impossible without it. Are you still with me here? I don't want to bore you to death before I get us to the kicker.

The fifth chakra is at the level of the throat, or voice box, and appropriately deals with mitigating all those necessarily powerful lower energies below it. With your heart chakra open, unblocking this chakra helps direct your instincts toward higher, more spiritual goals. It helps you find your voice. We use it to communicate truthfully in a way that's necessary for our spiritual release and expansion.

The sixth chakra is located between your eyebrows in the center of your forehead—what the swamis call the "Third Eye." This is the spot from which your highest, clearest vision emanates; from here, you can see life's truths with real understanding. It's your spiritual vista point, or observation deck, so to speak. All the wisdom you've collected helps you focus your higher vision from here, so it's critical to your process. Close your eyes in meditation, and this is the intuitive center and opening of light you may actually "see" *inside* your forehead.

Your *intuitive intelligence,* originating in the heart, emanates from here. In fact, if you've stayed with me this far, it's probably because your intuitive intelligence is allowing you to do so. Your intellect may have run off a long time ago. But between intuitive intelligence and open-heartedness, there's a whole different, alternative way to actually *think* in here somewhere that's far superior to the simple intellect alone, because it's connected to the medium of Love. Because of that, you can realize a much deeper understanding of Life than intellect alone can ever hope to give you.

The seventh, or crown, chakra is the portal naturally located right at the top of your head. It's like an antenna, or a "power plug" into the energy of the Universe. The point in, and out, of your essential higher Life energies. You may not experience it everyday—as you do some of your lower, more insistent chakras—but notice how, whenever you reference Heaven, transcendence, admirable behavior, or mastery of some kind, you always intuitively speak of it in terms of your "higher self," our highest motivations, or even of "taking it *up* a few notches."

So there's all the esoteric groundwork, and here's why it's important. This map of ourselves can help describe just where the blockages, obstacles, and obsessions that interfere with Life (and Love) flowing in and out of us are. While we work to free ourselves up spiritually, they are, at least, handy points of reference and, at best, the actual centers of those particular energies. In the same way that the seven deadly sins describe where we may "miss the mark," the seven chakras describe the targets and where we're aiming from, in a way. They're our personal benchmarks for self-examination—the intersections of our spirits' energy centers.

So to put it simply, when it comes to making the transitions of our lives—from childhood to adulthood; from confusion to wholeness; from isolation to connectedness; from being out of Love to being *in Love;* from "life" to "death"—it's good to have some awareness of these channels and their possible obstacles in order for our energies to move from one state of being to another. We'll want them to be as clear and as open as we can possibly get them.

Not having had any memorable experience of "life right before being born" in the way I've experienced what may come immediately afterward, I can't suggest a way for you to segué into your next life (though I'm sure there are some tricks to it). But, given all the information we've just covered, please bear with me as I venture a guess as to how it all may influence the process of (any) transition.

We know that first we have to clear our emotional obstacles out of the way, as well as we can. Tie up all of our loose ends; let go of our ego attachments; become open-hearted. And then, if we can muster the self-awareness, we'll want our spirits, unencumbered by any "lower-chakra baggage," to move from the heart through the crown chakra, our "vacuum tube" back to the Source. This is roughly what some ancient masters suggest is possible. Does it sound a little crazy? Maybe, but let me return you to my earlier point that *we are all on a tiny ball hanging in outer space,* which is still, as always, a sufficiently inspirational context for yours truly.

So many thousands of survivors of Near Death Experiences describe a passage out through the same "tunnel with the light at the end of it" that it's either an electrochemical brain phenomenon, or it's an actual path to our next life. Although I never saw that particular light, I hope it's obvious which path I'd take if I were you. No fussing around with argumentative brain-chemistry theories at that point; I'm only thinking about heading *straight into the light,* and reuniting with all that awaits us there.

Whether we regard these chakras as just interesting ways to symbolize characteristics of human nature, or if after centuries of searching, the monks and swamis have found a way to describe the actual spiritual mechanisms of Life, the point seems to be the same. We don't want to be stuck in the lower aspects of our physical selves at any time if we can help it—and particularly not at "the end," even if it just means living responsibly with as much Love and fulfillment as possible.

I'll bet that, when you sit quietly and focus on these chakra points as the centers of your Life energies, you can really feel each of them. That may certainly be true when it comes to your heart chakra being the center of Love and emotion; and it should also be so for your voice, "Third Eye," and crown chakras when it comes to the expressions of your intellect and your aspirations. So it's pretty easy to make sense of the idea that it's best to keep your lower energies secondary, at every stage of your life. Childhood imagination, high school insecurities, competitiveness, the desire for recognition, the desire to dominate, "scoring," and "winning" have all at times been necessary and useful motivations. But now you need to set all that aside, to allow your unfettered growth out beyond your personal barriers and limitations. Beyond the person (or people) that you have been, to that authentic person whom you have always been becoming. The person you really want to be.

Now we've tied up our loose ends, smoothed out our rough spots, made our restitution, and surrendered our self-importance to serenity, compassion, and Love. Hopefully, by living in a way that promotes and protects our eternal principles of happiness and fulfillment (in the eternal *now*), we haven't picked up any new baggage that we've got to get rid of. And of course, one hopes that we've already been skinny-dipping in the ocean of Love for some time now.

If we know we're about to leave this life, and we've got the awareness, we can start a kind of checklist for our spiritual release. As I suggested earlier, the level of the heart is where this energy really starts, so that's where you want to begin, once and for all, to set your baggage down and throw the door of your heart open to allow Love to lift and carry you. Try to ground your spirit at that heart level as consciously as you can, and humbly *ask* (God, Love, the

Universe, *whoever. . .)* to lift you up and release you from your physical desires and demands.

Next, move up to your voice box chakra and turn over all those systems of restraint and control, so that you can say whatever you have to say truthfully—right from the heart, if you feel you need to. Unload anything that carries inner weight, like a piece of advice to a friend or an expression of Love to a family member. Or something funny to anyone. Honesty and humor are eternally good ideas.

Then, stop and have a look around from the sixth chakra, the "Third Eye," if you can. Take a good look at Life, as it is and as it has been, using your highest vision. It's beautiful, and probably quite satisfying, no matter what. This calm, connected, *illuminated* place gives you the best and wisest view of your life that Life's wisdom can possibly give you. Humility earns you this vantage point.

Some of us lucky ones will have the pleasure, honor, and focused Love of those who have been closest to us gathered around. The rest simply have the pleasure of taking in the remarkable beauty of this Life all around us, even in its most mundane forms. I think this is the time when we have the chance to *see* the Source from this side, to realize that blissful *being-ness*. It's said that the way we see the Universe is the way the Universe sees us—and thank God the Universe is always serene, and *very* forgiving. At least I know it sure has been in my case.

From this place, we can see the course of everything— the roundness and completeness of the whole experience. In this grace-filled frame of mind, we can revisit any part of our lives without regrets and know that most of our troubles were caused all along by thinking we were separate, when in truth we come from everything and go back to everything. All of Life has always been part of us, and we've been part of it, all along. Even what seemed "bad" at the time wasn't really all that bad as we reframe our picture in this light. It was exactly what we needed.

*Now,* as always, is the best time to be grateful for everything this life has given you. It's all of it been exactly what you needed it to be. A *co-creation* that you can happily accept and take responsibility for the part you played in it. A co-creation that you can look forward to.

Here, I'd like to take a brief time-out from our process of dying to ask a pretty important question: *What life are we dying from right now?* What life do we need to "die" from? This process I'm describing isn't meant to be applied exclusively to our final moments of human life, you know; it may work very well for any life we need to "die" from, whether it's our last lives on planet Earth or not.

Most of us have experienced one or more of these transitions from one "life" to another—monumental life changes after which nothing could ever be the same. Often, these are due to some calamity, some personal catastrophe or self-realization that destroys "who we thought we were" and sends us into a whole new life of self-discovery. Carl Jung called it *individuation*—the process of finding out who you really are. Converted Christians may call it "being born again"—into the eternal spirit of Christ, that is. I call it being given a second chance at life—or in my case, a third and fourth.

When a life you're living simply doesn't work for you anymore, it may just be time to "kill" that self off. It may be time to use something like the process I've described in these pages to release your limiting expectations and definitions—your obstacles to the flow of Love (your "old" self)—and release your authentic, eternal self into a new way of living. It takes work to change and, by changing, to allow yourself to grow spiritually.

This is where just about everybody's favorite prayer, attributed to St. Francis of Assisi (the patron saint of animals, 1181–1226 CE) may come in handy to help describe the whole process in a nutshell. You may want to pay special attention to the last paragraph here, although all of it is about positive transformations:

Lord, make me a channel of thy peace
That where there is hatred I may bring Love,
That where there is wrong, I may bring forgiveness,
That where there is discord, I may bring harmony,
That where there is error, I may bring truth,
That where there is doubt, I may bring faith,
That where there is despair, I may bring hope,

That where there are shadows, I may bring light,
That where there is sadness, I may bring joy.

Grant that I may seek rather to comfort, than to be comforted,
To understand, than to be understood,
To love, than to be loved.

For it is by forgetting self that one finds *self*.
It is by forgiving that one is forgiven,
it is by dying that one awakens to eternal life.
Amen.

In this way, what we usually think of as dying really is a part of our larger lives. It always has been, and it always will be. It's that change we all have to make—we don't have any say-so, really. We have to do it to grow and to evolve spiritually. Passing physically from this life to the next is painful and difficult in the same way that passing from one life to another has always been. It's really not so bad, after all. In fact, it's a prized necessity.

And now we return to our previously scheduled program . . .

According to the wealth of human experience, the process of "exiting" can be a little like being down in a manhole and working your way up to an opening of light. It may seem comfortably familiar—even already known—the way so many survivors have described that trip into "the light." Without much choice, we simply let go, *surrender*, and humbly head off in the proper direction—without messing around along the way too much. Intuitively, we all know where to go.

I simply had never put myself in the right place. I didn't have my life in its proper order, or my lessons learned very well. I was always being knocked out of it blindly, from behind. Jerked out by the feet—or worse, kicked out by a skinhead. But thank goodness, you probably won't have to go through that. Perhaps you can be more aware, and be gently exonerated when your time comes, with some grace and ease.

So, without further knocking you over the head with it, the one thing that will make this (and any) surrender easy is, of course, Love itself. If you know that already, then it's the right time—anytime—to concentrate on the single most important expression of gratitude, which it can never hurt to keep present right out in front of our lives. Maybe it goes something like this:

Thank You, Universe, God, Divine Mother, loving ancestors, for this Life full of Love: for the joy and richness that I've experienced in it. All of it. I surrender myself to You now willingly with hope and gratitude in my heart. Release me

> from the troubles of this body. Help me to carry along all my Love, and for Love to carry me into whatever comes next. Thank you for this miraculous blessing of Life.

Or however you may be compelled to say it.

If we can keep the focus in our hearts on our personal concept of God and Love and light as much as possible—not just at our passing, but *all* the time—and if we can keep the focus on connecting to that Source, then we are on our way to Heaven. When we concentrate on all the Love we've had in our lives—on the Love we still have to give and to receive, and on the medium of Love in the Universe and all Creation—then we're in Heaven already. It's a pretty high bar to set, but (with a little help from our friends) it's a goal that everyone of us is designed to reach.

Hopefully, with gratitude in our hearts and beautiful intention on our path through the crown chakra, the elemental, eternal tide of Love will well up through our hearts and lift us up from beneath (or gently shepherd us along from behind. . .a little up and to the left). And we will be drawn up like a drop of water through a straw, right through and into that "light at the end of the tunnel."

Like it or not, we're carried by Love on out of this life into a blissful new freedom, and a new adventure beyond anything we've ever dreamt of, or could possibly have imagined. That's what happens. All you really need is Love.

If you are worried about "going to Hell," then maybe you should be. I can tell you (from experience, too) that Hell, anywhere, is a place where there is no Love. Where only the harsh realities of material life hold sway. If you've never allowed Love into your life—never felt as if it were as important as other things, or never felt yourself to be part of it—then you may know a little bit about Hell already. It's only in sincere and objective self-examination, where your past and your present and your future collapse into one moment wholly owned by Love, that you'll find your redemption and find real Life. It can happen in an instant, with a simple transmutation of your heart. With a simple *opening up.*

It's the same in all of Life, here and beyond, I believe. And all the human evidence and wisdom from all through the ages suggests that the redemption we seek to take us from Hell to Heaven, from lonely regret to blissful fulfillment, is all part of a pretty forgiving system. So it's all up to you. How free do you want to be?

I know that all this last "technical" part I've laid out may seem to be somewhat obscure and speculative. How can anyone know about the actual mechanism of the spirit leaving the body? Since I have accidentally experienced something like this in a less controlled way, I'm very prone to believe in where my intuitive intelligence leads me now. After all, many other people have had very coherent, very conscious experiences that describe exactly the same thing.

And you know, I do believe that all those trustworthy swamis and monks have, through sheer dedication and devotion to the Divine, really learned how to explore that "Eternal Consciousness" from their seat in *this* life—from a cushion right here on the floor. So if, incredibly, they can get *there* from *here* already, I'm quite sure that my limited peeks into the "after-world" (and those of so many others), could have been credibly attained by a few good clonks on the head. . .and that Heaven can most definitely be found by dying.

Of course you can, and should, simply close your eyes and honestly ask yourself in your heart: Is this stuff all true, or not? Then sit and really listen, and trust your own answer. In this way, intuitively, all of us already know everything we'll ever need to know, just as we already have everything we need to be happy.

If after that it makes any sense to you—this description of the trip out the other side—then no doubt that sense has arisen from the same place within you as it does within me—a place that is within all of us. I never had the chance to apply these wise old techniques myself (even my version of them), but I sure would like to the next time I get the chance. I think they could be a big improvement.

I got surprised by Life (and "death"), and yet even the unprepared-for experiences I had informed me of the amazing possibilities that live in us and await us all. And this has given me such a comfort, such a powerful hope, and such a profound understanding about where our potential (where Love) can take us that I've been compelled to pass it along to you with all my heart. You won't need to be surprised by how it all works; with your open heart, you can have faith. And hope. And grace.

When the sun sets in one place, it's rising in another.

That's why the circle symbolizes Life so well. It always comes back around. It contains everything. It describes everything. The Sun, the Earth, the moon, and their orbits; you and me and all of us, and our overlapping orbits. Nothing, wholeness, continuity, completion. Beginning, heading out, changing form, going out further, changing again and again, going all the way back around—and then rolling on around all the way back home.

How many times have we all experienced—how many times *will* we all experience—that cycle of Life? We just don't know . . . yet.

# How to Meet Anyone, Including Your Maker

Each day, you have some kind of plans for tomorrow, and you will have every day for the rest of your life—even if you expect tomorrow to be your "last." Or even if you don't. Go ahead and make your plans as if tomorrow were the day that you could be going on a trip, on an adventure—because that's basically what tomorrow is always like, in a way. You never know what may happen. You may find yourself suddenly moving into totally uncharted territory, even though you really thought you knew where you were. Or you may arrive someplace you've never been, only to find it impossibly familiar. Everything can always be other than what we expect it to be; in fact, that's the only expectation we're right to have.

When you set off on a trip, you never know just what you'll encounter. Some trips are easy; everything goes perfectly. Some are harder and full of unplanned-for discombobulations. The secret, of course, lies in being personally prepared for whatever may come, and in being happy with whatever that is, as it is.

On the trip through Life—from life *to* life—you really needn't worry too much about booking anything in advance. In a way, you've been booking it all along—and you can always make a last-minute change in direction, a different choice, if you need to. Then, if you're open to the unexpected, whatever travel arrangements may await you will be quite good indeed. The details of the trip may be unpredictable, but once you're on board, the ride can be effortless and comfortable, and will always end up taking you right where you need to be.

Remember trips you've taken before? (Not the business trips; this one's more for pleasure.) You may have stayed in some swanky hotels, and enjoyed some very fine dining and the like. All of which is great, but it's possible that your best memories were made when you happened off the beaten path and accidently stumbled into a place where the locals loved to hang out.

Nobody needed to know who you were "supposed to be" there, or really even cared much. You could just be your *self*. Your true self—ready to experience the hospitality, the camaraderie, the Love that the people there had to share. You probably didn't even have very much along with you— just a couple of bucks and some bumps and hiccups—but you were especially ready to see a world with new eyes and experience new and wonderful things. And so you did.

You may have made some lifelong friends. Maybe you had one of the greatest, most memorable times of your life, without ever having had any expectations about what was going to happen. Perhaps it was nothing that was ever supposed to happen. That's the beautiful anonymity of living a fully spiritual life. It doesn't matter who (or even where) *you're supposed to be*. Judgments aren't necessary. Nor comparisons. Nor expectations. Nothing ever needs to be proven, except your effort to live with Love and your willingness to keep growing. You never even really have to worry about today, or tomorrow—just always right *now*.

When you travel that way—simply and lightly, with humility and curiosity and open-heartedness—you're bound to discover the most beautiful things about yourself, about everyone else, and about Life. You learn the rewards of simply showing up and being the best person you know how to be, without expecting anything in return except maybe the chance to learn something new and to share a little Love.

If it's at all possible, can you make your "travel" plans *through* Life like that?

You'll never have to fear about not being "who you are"; you'll always be that. You needn't fear any end to your special and unique experience of *being;* each one of us will always experience that as well. Perhaps with fewer boundaries and distinctions between us. Maybe without these clunky encumbrances that we ride around in, as beautiful as they've always seemed to us. Or not.

Know that when you follow the path that we all intuitively know by heart—one where you don't need anything you may think you need—that you'll always have everything you need right there already. Wherever the heck *there* will be.

And you will always be you (only maybe *more so)*, and I will always be me, and all of us will always be all of us— and all of us will always be as we have always been. If you see me there, float on over on your cloud or whatever and introduce yourself. I'd love to get to know you better, even though I bet I already do.

Bless you, brothers and sisters
And . . . *Aloha!*

# Appendix
# Some Parting Thoughts

"Our concern must be to live while we're alive . . . to release our inner selves from the spiritual death that comes with living behind a façade designed to conform to external definitions of who and what we are."

Elisabeth Kübler-Ross

. . . and this from Rumi (1207–1273 CE):

"God does not look at outward forms, but at the Love within your Love."

# Acknowledgments

I'd like to express my heartfelt gratitude to Caroline Pincus of Red Wheel/Weiser Books and Conari Press for receiving an earlier version of this book with an open heart and mind, and for carrying enough faith to keep the door open for another couple years until it was ready. A very special thanks to Martin Rowe, of Lantern Books, for his generosity and encouragement, and for sending me to the right door in the first place.

The book didn't take all that long to write, but it was quite a stretch of road to reach the place where the words could be found. Along the way, I owe a debt of thanks to a number of people, not the least being my mother, Dorothy, for her enduring grace and ceaseless support. To my beautiful aunt, Ruth Moffett, whose guidance and protection kept me alive through thick and thin. To my longtime Zen compañero, Thomas Ingalls; my life mentors, Raymond Lewis and Don Weller; Doris Grumbach, Sybil Pike, and James Hillman; my eternal best man, T. M. Davidson; Leonard Koren; Richard Grossinger; the mobile Emergency Medical Services of the City of Tempe; the kind folks at *The Mindful Word*; and a special thanks to my deepest sounding board, Michael Goldbarg.

And of course to my extraordinary wife Sue; and my guardian angel, Anne.

In lieu of creating an ersatz bibliography of sorts, I'd like to thank the brilliant spiritual teachers, passed and present, whose talks and writings have made this world a place of miracles, and in keeping with that, helped to make this book possible:

Sri Aurobindo, Black Elk, Joseph Campbell, Pema Chödrön, His Holiness the 14th Dalai Lama, Wayne Dyer, Albert Einstein, Viktor Frankl, Mahatma Gandhi, Christopher Isherwood, William James, C.G. Jung, Louis Lapham, Ernst Laszlo, Jean-Yves LeLoup, Oren Lyons, Swami Prabhavananda, Ramana Maharshi, Juan Mascaró, Thomas Merton, Bill Moyers, Ravi Ravindra, Shunryu Suzuki, Rabindranath Tagore, Eckhardt Tolle, Chögyam Trungpa, Kurt Vonnegut, Swami Vivekananda, White Eagle, Marianne Williamson, and William Wilson.

Most of all to Yeshua, Buddha, Krishna, Lao Tzu, Patanjali, Rumi . . . and God.

And to you, dear reader, for keeping your mind and heart open, and remaining forever part of this miraculous journey.

# About the Author

David Turner

Robert Kopecky is an Emmy-nominated art director. He designed the credits for Showtime's *Weeds,* art directed *WordWorld* for PBS Kids, and has illustrated for *The New York Times, Sports Illustrated,* and many more. He contributes to *Evolver.net, NewBuddhist.com, TheMindfulWord.com,* and elsewhere. He lives in Brooklyn with his wife, Sue Pike, the Animal Talker (*SuePikeEnergy.com*).

Visit him at *http://RobertKopecky.blogspot.com.*

# To Our Readers

Conari Press, an imprint of Red Wheel/Weiser, publishes books on topics ranging from spirituality, personal growth, and relationships to women's issues, parenting, and social issues. Our mission is to publish quality books that will make a difference in people's lives—how we feel about ourselves and how we relate to one another. We value integrity, compassion, and receptivity, both in the books we publish and in the way we do business.

Our readers are our most important resource, and we appreciate your input, suggestions, and ideas about what you would like to see published.

Visit our website at *www.redwheelweiser.com* to learn about our upcoming books and free downloads, and be sure to go to *www.redwheelweiser.com/newsletter* to sign up for newsletters and exclusive offers.

You can also contact us at *info@rwwbooks.com*.

Conari Press
an imprint of Red Wheel/Weiser, LLC
665 Third Street, Suite 400
San Francisco, CA 94107